beyond the stained glass ceiling

Equipping & Encouraging Female Pastors

CHRISTINE A. SMITH

Foreword by Marvin A. McMickle

JUDSON PRESS
PUBLISHERS SINCE 1824

Join our mailing list for updates and special offers.
www.judsonpress.com/mailing_list.cfm

Library of Congress Cataloging-in-Publication data
Smith, Christine A.
Beyond the stained glass ceiling / Christine A. Smith.—1st ed. p. cm.
Includes bibliographical references. ISBN 978-0-8170-1727-9 (pbk.: alk. paper)
1. Women clergy—United States. I. Title.
BV676.S65 2013   262'.140820973—dc23
2012034318

Printed in the U.S.A.
First Edition, 2013.

To my Lord and Savior Jesus Christ
for granting me this wonderful opportunity.

To my husband, Aristide Smith Jr.,
for his unwavering love, encouragement,
and support over the years. Thank you
husband for making it possible for
me to do all that I do in the ministry,
by the grace of God,
being sure that we maintain
balance in our home life.

Also, to our three beautiful children,
Aristide III, Caleb, and Aris,
for sharing Mommy and supporting the vision.

CONTENTS

Foreword

A personal disclaimer might be in order before anyone reads the words that follow: I have known, supported, and believed in the ministry of Christine Smith long before this book had ever been conceived in her mind. The experience of reading *Beyond the Stained Glass Ceiling* was like reliving the questions and conversations we have shared over more than 15 years. I was the preacher at her ordination service, and I looked on with pride when she was installed as pastor of Covenant Baptist Church in Wickliffe, Ohio. I gladly served under her direction when she was president of the Cleveland Baptist Association. We served together on the Ministry Committee of that association where we and others on that committee debated and voted on the suitability of male and female candidates for ordination. I am not an outside reader offering a peer review. I am a friend and a colleague of Christian Smith, and as such I am deeply grateful that Judson Press has provided her with this platform both to share her story and to be a resource to other women who are beginning the journey on a trail that she has already blazed.

Beyond the Stained Glass Ceiling reminds me of the words that Hillary Clinton spoke after the 2008 Democratic Party Primary when she contested so effectively for the nomination for President of the United States. Barack Obama went on to win that nomination, an act made certain by then-Senator Clinton's decision to end her own presidential campaign and second the nomination for

Obama. Days later she spoke to her core supporters and said, "Although we weren't able to shatter that highest, hardest glass ceiling this time, it's got about 18 million cracks in it" (a reference to every vote she received in the state primaries). This book, *Beyond the Stained Glass Ceiling* will have a similar effect; if it does not shatter the ceiling that blocks women from entering into and advancing to larger congregations, it will shatter many of the obstacles that have stood in the way of women for so long.

This book does everything you would expect such a book to do. It points to the women in the Bible whose leadership, both in ancient Israel and in the early Christian church, often escapes attention. It offers moving testimonies of other women who, like the author, have had to persevere in the face of limited opportunities and excessive resistance. It discusses the dilemma of women that are so often faced both with ageism and sexism. Most painful of all, it reminds us that, while women have become the majority of the student body in many of the seminaries and divinity schools in the United States, they have to hold onto their sense of self-esteem and the certainty of their calling while local churches choose unqualified and less qualified men over well qualified women.

I hope multiple audiences will walk away from *Beyond the Stained Glass Ceiling* with a greater awareness of their own responsibilities concerning the aspirations of women to enter the ministry. Women who are looking to secure their first pastoral assignment will find great guidance and advice about how to navigate that process. Women who have already been called to a pastoral assignment but who are not being offered any future opportunities will find encouragement to keep serving faithfully where they are. Denominational leaders will discover that they bear a special responsibility when it comes to encouraging local churches under their supervision to embrace a woman as their senior pastor. Male pastors of local churches are encouraged to be open to the women in their churches who announce that God has called them into pastoral ministry. As Smith so effectively points out in this book, the early and continuing support of male clergy is an essential part of the process of tearing down the stereotypes, obstacles, prejudices and bad theology that has kept the stained glass ceiling in place for so long.

As Marilyn Parker Jeffries observes in this book, I have long believed that at the bottom of this problem is poor biblical exegesis. There is no doubt that given the patriarchal nature of the era in which the Bible was written that women would be excluded from many, if not most leadership roles. However, we have already moved beyond many of the cultural practices that were in force between thousands of years ago. We do not observe a kosher diet or sacrifice animals in worship. We do not stone disrespectful children or exclude people with disabilities from worship. Biblical interpretation done responsibly allows us to recognize that some parts of the Bible were the products of their own time, but were not necessarily meant to be enforced for all time.

So it is with the issue of women in ministry: it is not the Bible that limits women's opportunities, it is bad biblical interpretation. When people read *Beyond the Stained Glass Ceiling* and consider the biblical texts it highlights, it will not be long before the stained glass ceiling will crack and fall like the once-mighty walls of Jericho.

—Marvin A. McMickle, MDiv, PhD
President
Colgate Rochester Crozer Divinity School

Introduction

The concept of the glass ceiling is not new. In the secular realm, the glass ceiling represents the barrier that prevents qualified individuals from excelling beyond a certain level due to their race, gender, or orientation. For those of us who serve in the sacred or religious realm, we know it as the stained glass ceiling, referring to the barriers imposed by churches. About five years ago, during the Speak Until Justice Wakes conference (2008, ABCUSA) Rev. Kasey Jones, senior pastor of the National Baptist Memorial Church in Washington, D.C., and I began comparing notes about our experiences as female senior pastors. Out of that discussion grew a desire and decision to learn more about how other female clergy are faring as they pursue ministry opportunities or serve as senior pastors. We wanted to hear their stories—their challenges, victories, testimonies, and words of wisdom. In *Beyond the Stained Glass Ceiling: Equipping and Encouraging Female Pastors,* we celebrate the good news that God has opened the eyes of some congregants regarding the legitimacy and divine prerogative of God to call females to the holy vocation of pastoring. However, there is still much work to be done.

Contrary to some reports, female clergy have not yet arrived. While a few denominations such as United Methodists, the Presbyterian Church (USA), United Church of Christ, Disciples of Christ, and American Baptist Churches USA have accepted and called women to serve as senior pastors, many qualified and well-equipped sisters still struggle to have their gifts of preaching and pastoring recognized. Among those who have become senior pastors, remnants of the stained glass ceiling persist.

According to the Barna Group, women represent just 5 percent of all Protestant senior pastors. According to a 2008 *Christianity Today* article, this number has risen slightly to 9 percent.[1] However, female pastors are much more likely to be seminary-trained (86 percent have a seminary degree, compared with 60 percent of male pastors); are more than twice as likely to have been divorced (31 percent, compared with 12 percent among male pastors); have less experience in the pastorate (nine years in full-time paid ministry, compared with a median of seventeen years among men); last less time in a given church than do men (three years per pastorate, compared with almost six years among men); and receive much lower compensation.[2]

Historically, women have faced a variety of obstacles preventing them from being placed in the role of senior pastor. Theologically, women seeking to fill leadership roles in the church have been pummeled by misinterpretations of the writings of the apostle Paul. Paul's words to Timothy state: "Women should learn in silence and all humility. I do not allow them to teach or to have authority over men; they must keep quiet" (1 Timothy 2:11-12, GNB). This Scripture is a favorite tool of oppression. When used out of context, it appears to justify denying women leadership roles over men in general and pastoral roles in particular.

However, many Scriptures speak to the fallacies of this unfortunate use of the verses. For example, the army commander Barak would not go into war without the guidance and company of the judge and prophetess Deborah. In her position as judge, Deborah clearly had authority over women *and* men. Judges 4:4-9 (NIV) attests to this fact:

Now Deborah, a prophet, the wife of Lappidoth, was leading Israel at that time. She held court under the Palm of Deborah between Ramah and Bethel in the hill country of Ephraim, and the Israelites went up to her to have their disputes decided. She sent for Barak son of Abinoam from Kedesh in Naphtali and said to him, "The LORD, the God of Israel, commands you: 'Go, take with you ten thousand men of Naphtali and Zebulun and lead them up to Mount Tabor. I will lead Sisera, the commander of Jabin's army, with his chariots and his troops to the Kishon River and give him into your hands.'"

Barak said to her, "If you go with me, I will go; but if you don't go with me, I won't go."

"Certainly I will go with you," said Deborah. "But because of the course you are taking, the honor will not be yours, for the LORD will deliver Sisera into the hands of a woman."

Jael is the woman spoken of in Judges 4:9, and her story is found in Judges 4:18-23. The Old Testament writer of the book of Judges emphasizes the leadership roles of these two women, Deborah and Jael.

Other verses also show God's divine favor and endorsement of women in roles leading males and females. In Proverbs 31:1, King Lemuel's mother taught him with words of wisdom and guidance regarding selecting a wife: "The sayings of King Lemuel—an inspired utterance his mother taught him" (Proverbs 31:1, NIV). After the resurrection, Jesus appeared first to Mary Magdalene (Mark 16:9) and the other Mary, who went and told the disciples.

The apostle Paul wrote about Phoebe: "I commend to you our sister Phoebe, a deacon of the church in Cenchreae. I ask you to receive her in the Lord in a way worthy of his people and to give her any help she may need from you, for she has been the benefactor of many people, including me" (Romans 16:1-2, NIV). "Deacon" in this context refers to a Christian servant who works with the overseers or elders of a church. Similar uses of the term may be found in Philippians 1:1 and 1 Timothy 3:8, 12. The same term is applied to men serving in the deacons' ministry. No distinction is made between male and female servant-leaders. All of these scriptural examples make the interpretations forbidding women to teach or lead men inaccurate.

> **Today, female senior pastors can say, like James Weldon Johnson, "We have come over a way that with tears has been watered." However, women pastors do have reasons to rejoice.**

From a sociopolitical and cultural standpoint, women face opposition not only from men but also from other women. The comments of several female pastors we were privileged to interview bare this unfortunate fact (see chapter 3, "What Stands in Our Way?"). Today, female senior pastors can say, with echoes of James Weldon Johnson,[3] "We've traveled over a way that has been watered with tears." However, women pastors do have reasons to rejoice.

During the process of identifying female pastors of freewill denominations, I encountered several who serve large (500+), mid-sized (250+), and smaller congregations. The ranks of women serving as senior pastors are growing slowly. Their journeys are varied, their testimonies are compelling, and their insights are provocative.

So the questions arise: What can be done to shatter the stained glass ceiling for women clergy? What can we learn from those who have successfully burst through the barriers? How can we equip and encourage those who are seeking to become senior pastors?

What strategies should we develop in order to provide clear paths to success?

First, we must examine the lay of the land. In an attempt to identify and learn more about female pastors who have already broken through the stained glass ceiling, I developed and launched a survey of senior female pastors. (Although the many challenges and responsibilities of ministry caused Rev. Jones to decide to withdraw from the project, her initial work and partnership provided invaluable support to this effort.) I also conducted personal interviews and small-group sessions in which I asked specific questions related to the survey. The sample size was 150 female pastors. The research was limited to free will or autonomous denominations:

- American Baptist Churches USA
- Progressive National Baptist Convention
- National Baptist Convention of America, Inc.
- Cooperative Baptist Fellowship
- Southern Baptist Convention
- Full Gospel
- United Church of Christ
- Disciples of Christ
- Church planters/nondenominational

The survey, interviews, and small-group questions identified eight areas of examination: (1) personal information; (2–4) the ministry contexts in which women have been called as senior pastor; (5) the unique challenges that female clergy face personally and vocationally while pastoring; (6) personal stories that could give insight, encouragement, and cautions; (7) suggestions on how to increase conversations among clergy, laity, local congregations, regions, and denominational leaders regarding the acceptance of female pastors; and (8) suggestions about realistic strategies for increasing opportunities for female ministers to break through the proverbial stained glass ceiling.

Beyond the Stained Glass Ceiling speaks to female clergy who are seeking or are established in senior pastorates. It is also the hope to engage supporters and advocates in this conversation who will equip, encourage, support, and strategize on behalf of the women of God, seeking to "serve the present age, [their] calling to fulfill!"[4]

Notes

1. Jennifer Riley, "Charismatic Christianity in US—Myths Exposed," *Christianity Today*, January 8, 2008, http://www.christiantoday.com/article/charismatic.christianity.in.us.myths.exposed/16054.htm (accessed November 20, 2012).

2. "A Profile of Protestant Pastors in Anticipation of 'Pastor Appreciation Month,'" September 25, 2001, http://www.barna.org/barna-update/article/5-barna-update/59-a-profile-of-protestant-pastors-in-anticipation-of-qpastor-appreciation-monthq (accessed November 20, 2012).

3. James Weldon Johnson, "Lift Every Voice and Sing," in *Complete Poems* (2000).

4. Charles Wesley, "A Charge to Keep I Have," in *Short Hymns on Select Passages of Holy Scripture* (1762).

SECTION ONE

Breaking Through

CHAPTER 1

Whom Shall We Send?

And Mary said, Behold the handmaid of the Lord; be it unto me according to thy word. And the angel departed from her.
(Luke 1:38, KJV)

As we explore the question "Whom shall we send?" the example of Mary, the mother of Jesus, can provide great insight. Poor, young, unwed, and ordinary, Mary would not have been on the short list of most people to become the mother of the Messiah. Yet the Lord chose her. Readers of the text are left to speculate why the Lord chose Mary. We are given only the angel's words that she was "highly favored" and that the Lord was with her (Luke 1:28). Later, Mary expresses her own beliefs and words of praise regarding why she was chosen (Luke 1:46-55, KJV):

> And Mary said, My soul doth magnify the Lord,
> And my spirit hath rejoiced in God my Savior.
> For he hath regarded the low estate of his handmaiden:
>   for, behold, from henceforth all generations shall call
>   me blessed.
> For he that is mighty hath done to me great things; and
>   holy is his name.

> And his mercy is on them that fear him from generation
> to generation.
> He hath shewed strength with his arm; he hath scattered
> the proud in the imagination of their hearts.
> He hath put down the mighty from their seats, and
> exalted them of low degree.
> He hath filled the hungry with good things; and the rich
> he hath sent empty away.
> He hath holpen his servant Israel, in remembrance of
> his mercy;
> As he spake to our fathers, to Abraham, and to his seed
> for ever.

Clearly, Mary believed that God regarded her "low estate" and did "great things" to her. Mary praised God for exalting her and using her as an anointed vessel. Mary was chosen by God and sent forward to carry the Word that became flesh in the person of Jesus Christ. Understandably, upon receiving the message that God had chosen her, Mary had a question: "How can this be?" The angel provided a supernatural response to a natural question: "The Holy Ghost shall come upon thee, and the power of the Highest shall overshadow thee: therefore also that holy thing which shall be born of thee shall be called the Son of God" (Luke 1:35, KJV).

As women have heard and grappled with God's call upon their lives, many, like Mary, have asked, "How can this be?" Women are not supposed to preach and pastor. How can this be? I don't know any man who would license or ordain me. How can this be? I don't know what steps to take next. How can this be? I don't even know how to begin to explain what I am feeling. I don't have a lot, my name is not prominent, frequently I am overlooked, I'm not in the in-crowd, I'm not popular, people have even shunned me. Lord, how can this be?

At the appointed time, God sends angels to declare, "The Holy Ghost shall come upon you, and the power of the Highest shall overshadow you." God has many Marys to send. Will we recognize them? God's sending process is different from ours. Often we look for the best, the brightest, the most beautiful, the most popular, and that which is highly esteemed among people. God, however, uses a different barometer. God discerns the heart. The questions are: Will our hearts be open to the heart of God as God seeks to use us in the sending process? Will we allow ourselves to be the angels to help to clarify the call, provide reassurance, tell them that they are "highly favored" and held by God, and then send them forth to carry the gospel? We must believe that we are the angels— the women and men who affirm that God calls and chooses whomever God wills. Whom shall we send? We should send those who express and exhibit a willingness to say, like Mary, "be it unto me according to thy word."

Those who are called have to be open to the path that God places before them. Those who are sent must be realistic about the challenges ahead. It is important for those who do the sending to assist in the preparation process for those who are going and for those who will be on the receiving end. It is critical for the senders to teach those who are being sent that ministry is not for the faint of heart, whether male or female. I have heard many wise mentors declare, "If you can do anything else and be at peace, do it!" Many pastors can attest that there will be times when "the angel departs" and the sunset seems longer than the sunrise. There will be times when the only thing that provides sustaining power is the full knowledge and assurance that God has chosen you for this ministry, anointed and favored you for this journey, and brought you to the face of the earth for this purpose. While everyone needs encouragement and reassurance at times, all pastors must possess at the core of their being an unshakable conviction that God and God alone has called them. Anyone who lacks that certainty should not be sent.

Relative to the stained glass ceiling, the answer of who should be sent is greatly influenced by tradition, -isms (sexism, racism, classism, ageism), and misinterpretations of Scripture. The good news is that God is not bound by our traditions, -isms, or bad theology. The challenge, however, is cultivating an atmosphere, an environment, a new way of seeing God's hand and movement through and among whomever God chooses. Cultivating the field or the venues to which female pastors shall go is as important as preparing the pastors themselves.

Throughout *Beyond the Stained Glass Ceiling,* current realities are presented, as well as suggestions of how to expand opportunities for female pastors. In order to develop best practices or strategies for moving ahead, it is imperative to understand the background, current trends, and barriers that persist.

Background and Context

Over the last two decades, women entering the ministry and seeking ordination have steadily increased, particularly among denominations that have made the ordination of women official policy. The Unitarian Universalist Association has the highest proportion of ordained women at 30 percent. Closely following are the United Church of Christ, with approximately 25 percent, and the Disciples of Christ, with approximately 18 percent. The Free Methodists have the lowest proportion of women clergy, estimated at less than 1 percent.[1]

According to Edward C. Lehman Jr., the total amount of female clergy in most mainline Protestant denominations is 15 percent and in evangelical or fundamentalist groups about 7 percent.[2]

As we consider the sending process it is necessary to understand historical trends. It is important to examine the rugged road over which female clergy have traveled on the way to the pastorate, current descriptors of the pastorate for female clergy, and the trajectory for women in ministry desiring to become pastors if nothing changes.

Over the past few years, I have had the privilege of identifying and surveying female pastors of freewill denominations (churches that call rather than have appointed pastors). Conversations, interviews, and surveys were conducted with several female pastors of large (500+), mid-sized (250+), and smaller congregations. Each woman shared stories, experiences, and insights that can aid in further developing strategies for the advancement of women in ministry. Their examples also serve as powerful tools to encourage and equip female clergy seeking to become senior pastors. Samplings of the survey trends and results follow; the full survey is available online at www.judsonpress.com.

Trends Have Not Changed Much

A 2002 study by Lehman indicates that during the early to mid-1970s American Baptist Churches USA began a large movement of calling women to the pastorate. However, patterns rapidly emerged that revealed disparities between male and female pastors regarding initial placements and potential for future placements.[3] Eighty-eight percent of men were called to senior pastorates versus 49 percent of women. Eight percent of men were called to serve as associate or assistant pastors versus 27 percent of women. No men were called to serve as ministers of Christian education versus 5 percent of women.[4]

When these data are broken down by first, second, or third vocational placement, the gender differences remained clear. The percentages show a clear ascension for male clergy, advancing toward a larger pastorate or, if they were an associate minister, toward a solo pastorate. Women had lower levels of upward mobility.

Women were more likely to be called to serve as associate pastors or ministers or ministers of Christian education (see chart 1.1).

Chart 1.1: Placement as an Assistant or Associate Pastor		
	Men	**Women**
First job	32%	58%
Second job	15%	51%
Third-plus job	8%	40%

Source: Edward C. Lehman Jr., "Women's Path into Ministry: Six Major Studies," in *Pulpit and Pew Research on Pastoral Leadership Reports* Fall 2002 (Durham, NC : Duke Divinity School, 2002), 14–15.

Lehman's results show that clergy, like others, desire to move upward when seeking another position. The study also reveals that men and women generally moved to larger locations. However, gender differences seemingly affected the rate at which they were able to advance. Although they were larger, the churches to which women tended to move were still significantly smaller than the average male's new position. Men more easily moved into larger parishes than did women.[5]

The level from which one starts greatly affects the heights to which one rises and the amount of time it will take. The phrase "level the playing field" is used by educators as they seek to close the achievement gap between inner-city students and their suburban counterparts. Educators make the argument that children who are given fewer opportunities, inferior study materials, minimal funds, or large student-teacher ratio will experience great difficulty competing with students who receive the best of everything.

Students in the inner city are being asked to make bricks without straw. While inner-city youth, for example, are being taught on a third-grade level in the fifth grade, suburban youth are being taught on a third-grade level in the first grade. Unless something is changed, how will they ever catch up?

In the same way, clergywomen are frequently handicapped at level one. They spend years as an associate minister, rarely gaining the experience necessary to prepare them for a larger first pastorate. By the time they have an opportunity to pastor, they are usually older and cannot move due to employment or family obligations. Thus they have severely limited options and most probably will not have another opportunity to pastor elsewhere.

Paula D. Nesbitt outlines specific patterns that influence clergy placement in or call to various types of congregations. She uses the term "career trajectory," which refers to placement patterns from a person's initial job to the end of his or her work career or vocation. Nesbitt suggests that most clergy begin by working as a staff minister in a larger church or a pastor of a smaller congregation. Typically, the starting position greatly influences the trajectory for the ending position.

While men frequently have the opportunity to move from a small congregation or staff position to a mid-sized or large church and possibly an executive position with a denomination, women often remain in the associate minister position. I have observed this pattern in the area where I serve. It has almost become fashionable for churches to have female ministers as associates or on paid staff. Often they appear loved and revered by congregants and senior pastors. It may even seem as though discrimination against women in ministry has vanished. The struggle, however, remains. Those same churches that love and revere a female associate minister have stated in no uncertain terms that they do not want a woman to serve as the senior pastor. As vacancy after vacancy opened up in

our city, overrun with anointed, called, seminary-educated, experienced female clergy, our area executive minister was told time and
time again by pulpit committees (often populated by women), "We
don't want a woman pastor!" Due to the aforementioned career
patterns, women generally remain in subordinate positions or in
smaller churches.[6]

Nesbitt offers the following generalizations:

■ Both men and women have experienced less vertical mobility
than in previous generations.
■ The first five years of a clergyperson's career are critical for
upward mobility. The more opportunities a person has to move in
the earlier days of ministry, the higher the level of placement
toward the end of ministry.
■ First positions clearly influence future opportunities. Men, more
than women, tend to obtain initial ministry positions that increase
the likelihood of vertical mobility.[7]

Nesbitt compared men and women regarding their career trajectory (see chart 1.2).

Chart 1.2: Career Trajectory among Pastors[8]		
Placement	Men	Women
more than 300 members	56%	5%
declining membership	29%	87%
multiple staff	41%	10%
aged 56 or older	39%	48%
college graduates	51%	30%
income $25,000+	50%	17%
high-status occupation	66%	47%

Regarding the data, Lehman states:

> Far more than the men, the women clergy find themselves
> in remote communities with small congregations contain-
> ing proportionately large numbers of older members pos-
> sessing fewer financial and cultural resources for their
> church programs. Such placements are not the stuff of pas-
> tors' dreams. Most men placed in such marginal situations
> discover that it is but a temporary step en-route to more
> desirable charges.
>
> Not so the women, who report that they feel "locked in."
> For more of those women than for men, the next move is
> either resigning to obtain more education for other forms
> of ministry or deciding to leave the ministry altogether.[9]

Lehman's study further explored obstacles to women's advancement. Some clergywomen felt that their own shortcomings and
lack of resources hindered them. Others believed that family
dynamics or responsibilities stood in the way of their advancement.
Most, however, believed that sexism played a dominant role in
their stagnation (53 percent).[10]

When asked about the coping mechanisms they used to overcome the perceived obstacles, women responded that they sought
support from others, worked to make adjustments (in attitude,
expectations, vision), sought counseling, and engaged in rituals
(patience, increased efforts, focused prayer).[11]

**The best predictor of success in placement
is a realistic placement strategy that
takes advantage of structures that link
candidates with churches.**

As female pastors are confronted with the realities of sexism and closed doors, there may be times when we question our life's purpose or a specific goal or direction. When knocked-upon doors remain closed, when detour signs keep popping up, when projects fail and dreams fall flat, we are confronted with the daunting question, "Whose no is it?" We are well acquainted with the Scriptures that tell us, "The steps of a good man [woman] are ordered by the LORD" (Psalm 37:23, KJV), "Delight thyself also in the LORD, and he shall give thee the desires of thine heart" (Psalm 37:4, KJV), and "In all thy ways acknowledge him, and he shall direct thy path" (Proverbs 3:6, KJV). But when the path keeps winding and the glimmer of light becomes dim, we keep asking ourselves, "Whose no is it?"

- When you've been to seminary and served faithfully in the lay ministry but for some reason still can't get ordained;
- When you've jumped through all of the hoops and prepared yourself well for pastoral search committees yet, as a woman, you still don't receive a call to pastor a church;
- When the men around you are less qualified yet continue to advance through several opportunities to pastor churches (while you remain in the same place);
- When you've applied to doctoral programs and aren't accepted;
- When you can't find a job;
- When you can't find a mate;
- When you can't seem to get to where you want to go

You are confronted with the question, "Whose no is it?"

Your answer to that soul-searching question will mean the difference between dogged pursuit of your dream, goals, and aspirations and bowing in humble submission. For those seeking a breakthrough, I offer the following encouragement: Through prayer and discernment, fasting and consulting, Spirit-led mentors and friends, strive to make a distinction between the reasons. In other words, is the no answer due to human sinfulness such as sexism, racism, ignorance, or mean-spiritedness on the part of those giving the answer? Or is the locked door, no matter the situation, God's decision to move your life into a different direction? Having the answer to that question is critical.

Understanding the origin of the no determines the strength of your pursuit. If you know beyond a shadow of a doubt that the Lord God Almighty has placed a vision, a dream, a call, a ministry within you, no devil in hell or human on earth can thwart your determination to attain that goal. God plus you are a majority! No weapon formed against you will prosper, and you will ultimately gain the victory. God will open doors that no one can shut and close doors that no one can open. God's voice and Holy Spirit will compel you to pursue doggedly, and ultimately you will overcome.

If, however, in your innermost being you have heard the Lord say, "My child, that is not my way for you," or "This is not the right time for you," or "I have something different for you," or "Stop!" and because of stubbornness, pride, foolish ambition, or misguided thoughts you keep going in the wrong direction, you will not prosper in your pursuits. When you reach the proverbial fork in the road and ask yourself if you should continue pursuing a particular goal or if you need to let it go, understanding the origin of the no means everything. Before deciding either way, before allowing naysayers to discourage you or well-meaning friends to encourage you to follow a path that is not the path the Lord has ordered for you, go before the Lord and stay there until the answer comes.

Lehman suggested that the best predictor of success in placement is a realistic placement strategy that takes advantage of structures that link candidates with churches.[12] This recommendation is not antithetical to prayer and faith. Prayer, wise counsel, and keen awareness of networking possibilities all go hand in hand. The data show that women who move beyond identifying barriers and coping mechanisms to developing placement strategies and finding ways to utilize the system to their advantage experience greater success. Lehman's data establish a troubling fact: The patterns of advancement for women in ministry have not changed much. The trends and results from the ABC Female Pastor survey (2009–2011) yield similar results:

■ The average age for women called to their first pastorate is between 40 and 49.
■ The majority of female senior pastors are Anglo American (63.8% surveyed).
■ The majority surveyed work thirty or more hours per week (61.1%).
■ The average salary was between $26,000 and $45,000.
■ The majority receive a housing allowance or are provided a parsonage.
■ This was the first pastorate for more than half of the women surveyed.
■ Pastoring was a new career path for most (second career/vocation).
■ The majority (68.8%) are married.
■ The average congregation size is between fifty and one hundred (39.7%; 32.1% 50 or less).
■ The average age of congregations was fifty-six or older (43.71%).
■ The congregations pastored by female clergy tend to be Anglo American (65.81%)[13]

Conclusions

Currently, most women called to pastor a Baptist congregation will receive their first (and frequently only) opportunity between the ages of forty and forty-nine. This is a critical factor because many churches are discouraged from calling pastors who are near the age of fifty. The thinking is that a younger pastor is needed to attract a younger demographic. Even pastors who have exhibited support for female clergy often, upon announcing their retirement, tell their congregations to pursue a younger candidate. With such instructions, they eliminate many excellent female candidates. Because most mid-sized to larger churches require a candidate to have at least five years' experience as a senior pastor and to have led a congregation of 250 members (and in some cases 500) or more, most female candidates are automatically disqualified. If a woman is called to any church, she will probably remain in that church throughout her pastoring vocation or make a lateral move to a similar congregation.

Since many female clergy are not licensed or ordained until later in life, due to circumstances (waiting for a male pastor to have his thinking transformed or for a congregation to give approval) rather than choice, the likelihood of them being called to pastor a reasonably healthy, established congregation significantly decreases. Those who are called to pastor a Baptist church will more than likely pastor an Anglo American congregation. For female clergy of other ethnicities, this is sometimes a challenging but necessary part of the process. With few exceptions, African American clergywomen will find most opportunities to pastor in Euro American congregations. In a perfect world, race and culture may not matter, but we do not live in a perfect world.

At the onset, both pastor and people may be willing to work together; both, however, may wrestle with the fact that they would like to have it another way. According to the ABC Female Pastor Survey, approximately 65 percent of clergywomen will pastor an Anglo American congregation. Some might retort, "We should not be concerned about race—we are all God's children, and heaven is diverse!" Nevertheless, diversity should be an intentional goal that is sought out of a vision and passion for racial and cultural reconciliation, not the result of two parties that have few other choices.

For minority female clergy who have been brought up, nurtured, loved, and supported by churches of their own culture, the pain of rejection after announcing the call to pastor, coupled with the fresh struggles of pastoring and compounded by the realities of cultural differences, can be daunting. Often, major differences exist in perceptions of leadership ("shepherd" versus "hireling"), administration (pastor as visionary and leader versus pastor as chaplain, subject to the direction and decisions of a congregational president, moderator, or board), and worship styles (call and response versus quiet contemplation; gospel and praise music versus traditional hymns and stoic styles; verbal expression versus silence). It can be very discouraging. Yet, in a deep desire to fulfill her calling, many a clergywoman will press through the challenges, make the most of what she has, and cultivate something beautiful. If individuals are honest, however, the ugliness of deep-seated prejudices can make crossing the hurdles of cultural diversity tricky. A pastor may experience that the church has a burst of growth, numerically, financially, and culturally, only to have that growth cancelled by an exodus from those made uncomfortable by what is perceived as a potential power shift. She may start with thirty, have fifty join, have twenty die (because many clergywomen will be called to congregations where the age range is from sixty-five to ninety), and have thirty decide to leave. She's suddenly back to thirty members!

If the church confronts the realities of current trends, explores them, and seeks to understand their origins and implications, it can then strategize to bring about change.

While this scenario appears hopeless and depressing, it should be viewed another way. If the church confronts the realities of current trends, explores them, and seeks to understand their origins and implications, it can then strategize to bring about change. The desired change is not to ensure that every female pastor is called to serve a large congregation, but rather to nurture environments that create expanded options for women. Some are called to serve in smaller venues. Others are called and equipped to lead in larger settings. Doors need to be opened for both. The experiences, testimonies, and words of wisdom provided by the many women and men serving in ministry, as well as advocates of female clergy, will help church leaders to implement effective plans to change the tide. The long, dark night of blocked opportunities will give way to the morning light when determination, prayerful planning, and courageous stands are taken by God's people. "Weeping may endure for a night, but joy cometh in the morning" (Psalm 30:5, KJV).

Notes

1. Edward C. Lehman Jr., "Women's Path into Ministry: Six Major Studies," in *Pulpit & Pew Research on Pastoral Leadership Reports,* Fall 2002, (Durham, NC): Duke Divinity School, 4.

2. Lehman, "Women's Path into Ministry," 4.

3. Lehman, "Women's Path into Ministry." 14–15.

4. Lehman, "Women's Path into Ministry." 14–15.

5. Lehman, "Women's Path into Ministry," 15.

6. Paula D. Nesbitt, *Feminization of the Clergy in America,* 55; Lehman, "Women's Path into Ministry," 18.

7. Nesbitt, *Feminization of the Clergy in America,* 18.

8. Nesbitt, *Feminization of the Clergy in America,* 55.

9. Lehman, "Women's Path into Ministry," 19.

10. Lehman, "Women's Path into Ministry," 19.

11. Lehman, "Women's Path into Ministry," 19.

12. Lehman, "Women's Path into Ministry," 18–19.

13. ABC Female Pastor survey (2009–2011), www.judsonpress.com/Free_download_book_excerpts.cfm.

CHAPTER 2

Where Shall We Go?

"This is my command—be strong and courageous! Do not be afraid or discouraged. For the LORD your God is with you wherever you go." (Joshua 1:9, NLT)

As Joshua prepared to enter the Promised Land, the Lord spoke specific words of instruction to prepare and encourage him for what he was about to face. The Lord spoke those words to Joshua because the path to the Promised Land was not easy. The Israelites would face giants, opposition from within their own ranks, days of discouragement, and times of feeling abandoned. As they faced various kinds of opposition, God wanted them to look beyond the struggle and through faith pursue the promises. As women consider the places that are frequently opened for them to enter as pastors, the same words are appropriate for them.

The places in which women find themselves being called to pastor may not be readily viewed as the promised land. The promises of God, however, are present in each situation, and women are moving with strength, courage, grace, and faith while holding fast to the confidence that God is with them. Of the one hundred or so women pastors surveyed, most serve churches with similar characteristics that are described in this chapter.

Characteristics of Calling Congregations

Passionate about Social Justice
Broadly speaking, liberationist churches and denominations are more open to female pastors. They tend to view social justice issues as a centerpiece of their understanding, interpretation, and application of Scripture. Their theology, at least in theory, includes freedom from gender bias. While challenges still remain in terms of the places within these denominations where women are placed or called, opportunities for female pastoral leadership do exist.

The exception, however, is historically African American churches that, despite liberationist views about racial inequality, tend to maintain a conservative attitude toward females serving as senior pastors. In fact, according to Aldon D. Morris and Shayne Lee, "The Black Baptist denominations along with the Church of God in Christ are the most conservative with respect to gender inequality especially as it relates to the ordination of women."[1]

In 1992, several female seminarians, along with myself, were interviewed for the article "Black Women Trying to Reach Pulpits Face Resistance: Clergy: Number of seminary students is on the rise, but some find the ministry in African-American culture remains a bastion for men" (*The Los Angeles Times*, Religious News Service, November 7, 1992). The article highlights the challenges African American women face as they exit seminary and pursue pastoral ministry.[2]

> Black women are flocking to seminaries across the country, but when they graduate they face a harsh reality. Ministry in the African-American culture remains a bastion for men.
>
> Some, such as the Rev. Gloria Bennett, have horror stories to tell.
>
> Bennett recalls that a middle-aged man politely accepted a church flyer from her last month at a shopping center in

Stockbridge, GA. But when she extended her hand and introduced herself, using her title, he snatched his hand back and screamed: "Don't touch me. You're a demon. God doesn't want women in the pulpit. A woman can never be over a man."[3]

To understand the venues that call female pastors, it is important also to understand those that will not. For a variety of reasons (see chapter 3, "What Stands in Our Way?"), minority clergywomen in general and African American clergywomen in particular experience great difficulty finding acceptance in churches of their own culture. Although many African American women enter the ministry and prepare themselves by attending seminary, they frequently experience rejection from historic black Baptist churches. Throughout the aforementioned article, examples are provided that support the unfortunate reality. The late Rev. Dr. James Costen shared his frustration as president of Atlanta's predominantly black Interdenominational Theological Center (ITC), where a third of the students are women, by suggesting that many churches would rather call an unqualified man than a super-qualified woman.

Dr. Jacquelyn Grant, a professor of womanist and systematic theology at ITC, expressed similar frustration by suggesting that black women view black men as the victims of oppression, therefore black women don't want to be insensitive to their inequitable treatment by unseating them as leaders in the church. Sadly, women are not beneficiaries of that reciprocal sensitivity. Dr. Grant further suggests that men and women have been socialized to think that women do not belong in leadership positions.

An ITC graduate from the late 1970s, Rev. Dr. Claudette Copeland, who is co-pastor with her husband of New Creation Christian Fellowship in San Antonio, Texas, suggested that sexism in the black church is both sociological and cultural. While there is affirmation of the strength of the black woman, black male preachers "guard their pulpits because the church has been the one place of authentic ownership for the black male."[4]

Many of the challenges cited in 1992 still exist. A 2011 *Gospel Today* article by Darryl Izzard emphasized the rigid stance regarding women in ministry in the Southern Baptist Convention: "Many mainstream denominations like the Southern Baptist Church are clear and very firm on their position regarding this issue. Their statement of belief reads: 'While both men and women are gifted for service in the church, the office of pastor is limited to men as qualified by scripture.'"[5]

One historically African American denomination, the African Methodist Episcopal (AME) Church, has made great strides toward calling women to higher levels of leadership. In 2000, the AME shattered a stained glass ceiling for women in ministry with the appointment of Rev. Dr. Vashti McKenzie as the first female bishop of the AME Church. Since that time, several more women have been appointed as bishops.

United Methodist, Disciples of Christ, United Church of Christ, Presbyterian, ELCA–The Evangelical Lutheran Church in America, Cooperative Baptist, and American Baptist Churches USA denominations have been the most receptive to women in pastoral leadership positions. Frequently, women who are refused licensure or ordination in their own denominations turn to these denominations for acceptance and credentialing. Some have achieved licensure and even ordination but still are blocked from becoming senior pastors. A *New York Times* article frames the issue:

> Women now make up 51 percent of the students in divinity school. But in the mainline Protestant churches that have been ordaining women for decades, women

account for only a small percentage—about 3 percent (according to one survey by a professor at Duke University) of pastors who lead large congregations (those with average Sunday attendance over 350). In evangelical churches, most of which do not ordain women, some women opt to leave for other denominations that will accept them as ministers. Women from historically black churches who want to ascend to the pulpit often start their own congregations.[6]

Founded by a Woman

Another common characteristic of calling congregations is that the church was founded by a woman. Several of the African American female pastors surveyed exemplify this reality: they are church planters. In an interview, Rev. Jacquelyn Ragin Olds, founder and senior pastor of Run with Endurance Ministries, spoke about some of the benefits and challenges of church planting.

> The benefits of church planting are freedom and autonomy. We can be creative. We had a chance to build from the ground up—have a fresh start from its inception. We are completely mobile—without a building, ministering much like the disciples. We are outside in the community like Jesus was.
>
> The challenges: trial and error—good sometimes and not good sometimes! Also staying focused is a challenge. We come up with a lot of good ideas, but we have to stay focused on the vision so that we don't wander off on every good idea. Also management can be a problem at times. Because we are creating as we go there are not a lot of rules. Sometimes we have to bear with the growing pains.
>
> Finances are a benefit and a challenge. Our overhead is very low, but at the same time trying to save up to move

into another place is going rather slow. It is has been a slow process. Fortunately, we are not in a hurry.[7]

More often than not, church planting for women is an outgrowth of closed doors in the traditional church venue.

More often than not, church planting for women is an outgrowth of closed doors in the traditional church venue. Church planting has several benefits. A pastor who plants a church has a certain level of autonomy. In other words, the pastor has the freedom to guide, shape, and shepherd the congregation as she envisions and as the Holy Spirit leads. She is free from the baggage of old, dysfunctional systems that may have developed over time in some traditional settings. As stated by Rev. Ragin Olds, the pastor is free to be creative in terms of ministry development, location, and congregation building. Challenges may include minimal financial resources, difficulty establishing a perception of legitimacy, few seasoned leaders, and finding a stable place to meet (lacking a church facility). All in all, some female ministers believe the pros outway the cons and make the determination to step out in faith and plant a church.

Another church planter, Apostle Dr. Mamie J. Harris Smith, founder and senior pastor of New Generation Christian Fellowship, shares her experiences in this interview.

CS: At what age did you first hear a call to the ministry?
MHS: I heard the call of God at age twelve (1957).
CS: Did you share your call experience with anyone? If so, how did they respond?
MHS: No. At that time, I was in a Methodist church. It was shortly after I heard God's call that a female pastor came and

preached at our church. After she preached, she prayed for me and laid hands on me. It was like a bolt of lightning. I was slain in the Spirit. My parents did not understand. They said that ever since the lady laid hands on me, I was different. From that day forward, I was moved by the Holy Spirit and knew that my life was different.

CS: How long did it take after acknowledging your call to become licensed or ordained?

MHS: It wasn't until 1990 that I acknowledged my call to my pastor, who happened to be my husband. He did not license me until 1992. He originally did not believe in women preachers. During that time God gave me peace and I served faithfully. I taught Sunday school and served in the church.

In 1987 I started Victorious Women's Fellowship. My husband saw the fruit of my labor, and it helped him to believe that I was called. Although my husband believed, the deacons did not feel that a woman should be preaching. They would not allow me to have the ministry meet in the church, so I began to go to hotels and rent space.

Whatever I was asked to do—read a Scripture, read the obituary, I read to the best of my ability with power and passion. If called upon to emcee programs, I would go. I was even asked to speak at the widows' banquets. I knew nothing about being a widow at the time. The Lord brought to mind the word, "Don't despise small beginnings."

CS: How did you decide to start your own church?

MHS: I didn't decide. God told me to feed his sheep. In 1996, my husband ordained me at the church where he had pastored for seventeen years. Six months later, he died of a massive heart attack. A young man and minister who I helped recruit to the church under my husband's pastorate was called to become the new pastor. I sat on the pastoral search committee and supported the calling. We never thought to ask him if he believed in female ministers because I was instrumental in bringing him to the church and he worked alongside me with my husband.

Interestingly, after he was called to serve as the senior pastor, he suddenly did not believe in women preachers. Shortly thereafter, I left and started my own ministry. He eventually licensed and ordained his own wife.[8]

The struggles described by these two pastors are representative of the stories of many African American female clergy who launched church ministries, swimming upstream to respond obediently to God's call upon their lives.

Additional Characteristics

This chapter has addressed some of the common demographics of churches with women senior pastors, but there are a few others. The majority of women surveyed were called to pastor churches with the following characteristics.

Churches in urban or suburban areas. These churches tend to be smaller and more comfortable with women in leadership roles. In urban and suburban areas, perhaps with smaller populations or underserved populations, churches may see women operating more prominently in leadership roles. In these areas, women may lead the household, make up the majority of educational structures or circles (PTA, teachers, small-group leaders, social networking clubs), and therefore be more readily accepted as pastors.

First female to pastor their particular church. Many of the churches that call female pastors do so out of necessity. Often the members are elderly, the offering has dropped, weekly attendance is small, and resources are minimal. Male pastors have long since left many of these churches. Frequently, lay leaders (predominantly women) will have filled in until a pastor comes. This factor may play a role in an evolving receptivity to a female pastor.

Churches with declining or dying membership. Female clergy are more likely to answer a call to these churches, seeing the call as an opportunity because few solo pastor options exist. Although historically men have also served as bi-vocational pastors of small congregations, more often than not they have chosen to and were not relegated to serve in those areas. The majority of men, however, less frequently accept churches with these demographics.

Churches that would have preferred a male pastor. Churches facing such difficulties often are unable to attract male pastors with wives and children. Men are unlikely to accept these churches for reasons of economics (being the primary bread winner) or career path (serving a small, dying church would take too long to revive, blocking them from their next perceived career step). More will be said about these factors in chapter 3, "What Stands in Our Way?" and chapter 5, "What Will We Find There?"

The Exceptions

Although there remain a number of freewill denominations that have reservations about calling female pastors, particularly those in African American communities, exceptions do exist. Among the exceptions, a specific factor stands out: In most instances, women called to lead larger congregations have been recommended and strongly supported by male predecessors or mentors.

Rev. Dr. Gina Marcia Stewart, senior pastor of Christ Missionary Baptist Church in Memphis, Tennessee, was baptized and mentored for ministry by her predecessor and former pastor, Rev. Eddie L. Currie. In 1995, she was elected by majority vote to serve as pastor of Christ Missionary Baptist Church. Since she became pastor, more than four thousand members have joined the church. According to the church website, Dr. Stewart is the first African American female elected to serve an established African American Baptist congregation in Memphis and Shelby County.[9]

In 1991, Rev. Dr. Wilma R. Johnson was called to pastor the New Prospect Missionary Baptist Church in Detroit, Michigan. Prior to being called to New Prospect, Dr. Johnson served as an assistant pastor at Hartford Memorial Baptist Church, where Rev. Dr. Charles Adams Sr. is senior pastor.[10] It should also be noted that New Prospect Missionary Baptist Church is affiliated with the National Baptist Convention, an African American body of Baptists that next to the Southern Baptist denomination is least likely to endorse a female pastor. Under Dr. Johnson's pastorate, the church has grown from approximately one thousand members to well over three thousand, according to the church website.

In 2009, Rev. Leslie Callahan was elected the fifth senior pastor of the historic St. Paul's Baptist Church in Philadelphia. Dr. Callahan is the first female pastor elected to serve this historic African American Baptist church in its 119-year history.[11] Although her calling to the church was not tied to the influence of her predecessor, she had the strong support of prominent male clergy, including her pastor, Rev. Albert Campbell, pastor of Mt. Carmel Baptist Church in Philadelphia, and Rev. Dr. J. Alfred Smith Sr., pastor emeritus of Allen Temple Baptist Church of Oakland, California.

In most instances, women called to lead larger congregations have been recommended and strongly supported by male predecessors or mentors.

The preceding references are made not to suggest that doors easily flung open for these women. Each distinguished herself as a well-educated, hardworking, well-qualified, anointed preacher and teacher of the gospel and as a visionary in her own right. Not to be underestimated, however, was the role that male clergy played in helping to carve out the paths that led to their election as senior pastors of historically African American Baptist churches.

Interim Ministries Help to Open Doors for Female Pastors

In general, interim ministers are asked to serve a church while the church is in the process of searching for a new pastor. Some churches and denominations have specific rules or guidelines that forbid an interim from becoming a candidate or being called to serve as the permanent pastor. However, some churches, after having spent many months or even years with an interim, will make the decision that the individual meets the needs of the congregation. A survey respondent shares her experience:

> I was surprised by the journey that led me here. I never wanted to be a pastor. I became a Christian ed director first. I started seminary because I was told I should if I were going to work as a professional. I never considered a pastorate until the church's committee asked me to take the position. I only took an interim position originally. After two years in the position, the church search committee asked me to take the position. They never interviewed anyone else. —*Pennsylvania*

Serving as an interim or pulpit supply person for a time can provide administrative, preaching, teaching, and relationship experience that can be used to build up a résumé as well as a proven record for leadership abilities. These positions also provide exposure to congregations, groups, and individuals who may not have otherwise had an opportunity to hear the minister. An added benefit is the strengthening of skills in all of these areas.

Where shall we go? Although opportunities to become a senior pastor remain limited for clergywomen, the suggestions in this chapter can help to broaden your thinking and increase your awareness of roads leading to the pastorate.

■ *Survey the land.* In other words, take time to prayerfully look over all of the opportunities available. Opportunities do exist. You have to be open and creative.

■ *Understand that you may have to serve a church of a different culture.* Doors may open more quickly for you if you are open to this option.

■ *Prayerfully consider becoming a church planter.* Explore denominational resources that may be available to assist in such an endeavor.

■ *Learn about interim ministries.* If you are so inclined, give it a try. Talk to denominational leaders about opportunities available in this area.

■ *Pray.* Walk in obedience to the Spirit of the Lord. Remain faithful in your current venue. Serve the Lord with gladness. Resist anger and bitterness. Be ready to move when the time is right.

"Be ye also ready!" (Matthew 24:44, KJV).

Notes

1. Shayne Lee and Aldon D. Morris, "The National Baptist Convention: Traditions and Contemporary Challenges" (research paper, Northwestern Reserve University, March 1, 2009), 3.

2. "Black Women Trying to Reach Pulpits Face Resistance: Clergy: Number of seminary students is on the rise, but some find the ministry in African-American culture remains a bastion for men," *The Los Angeles Times* (The Religious News Service), November 7, 1992, http://articles.latimes.com/1992-11-07/local/me-1309_1_black-women (accessed November 21, 2012).

3. "Black Women."

4. "Black Women."

5. Darryl Izzard, "*Gospel Today* Returns with a Cover Featuring Dynamic Women Pastors," GospelToday.com, January 9, 2011, http://mygospeltoday.com/?p=2444 (accessed November 21, 2012).

6. Neela Banerjee, "Clergywomen Find Hard Path to Bigger Pulpit," *New York Times*, August 26, 2006, www.nytimes.com/2006/08/26/us/26clergy.html?pagewanted=all (accessed November 21, 2012).

7. Christine A. Smith, *Shepastor*, "Testimony of a Church Planter," interview with Jacquelyn Ragin Olds, July 14, 2010.

8. Christine A. Smith, interview with Mamie J. Harris Smith, Griffin, GA, November 2011.

9. Christ Missionary Baptist Church, http://www.christmbc.org/senior_pastor.htm (accessed November 21, 2012).

10. New Prospect Missionary Baptist Church, http://www.newnpmbcunity.org/about—np/index.html (accessed November 21, 2012).

11. Press release, St. Paul's Baptist Church, September 9, 2009.

CHAPTER 3

What Stands in Our Way?

So God created humankind in his image, in the image of God he created them; male and female he created them.
(Genesis 1:27, NRSV)

Women in pursuit of a senior pastorate may encounter a number of obstacles. (Specific tips on key questions to ask in an interview or research to conduct before accepting a pastorate are offered in chapter 6, "Who Shall We Become There?") Scripture is often taken out of context and used to prevent women from serving as church leaders. Consider just a few of the ways Scripture is used to justify the second-class status of women in the church:

■ Women are blamed for the fall of humanity (Genesis 3:1-13).
■ Women are portrayed as sexual predators (Genesis 19:30-36; Judges 16; 1 Kings 11).
■ Women are depicted as deceitful and untrustworthy (Genesis 39:7-20).
■ Women are suspected of fornication or adultery (Deuteronomy 22:13-21; Numbers 5:11-31).
■ Women are silenced for stepping out of place in the church (1 Timothy 2:11-14).

Frequently, persons who draw on these passages to argue against women clergy ignore the broader implications of the texts. Much work has been done to refute the misinterpretation of these and other Scriptures that have been cited to prevent women from serving as pastors and church leaders.[1] Rather than rehashing these arguments, it is beneficial to consider other compelling Scriptures that speak positively about women in leadership roles within the church.

A number of women in Scripture are given the title of prophet. These women provided leadership, guidance, instruction, and words of warning to men, women, and entire nations. In Scripture, prophets speak on behalf of God, offering special words of wisdom, insight, confrontation, correction, and, in some instances, warnings that God wants communicated to God's people. Female prophets named in the Old Testament include Huldah (2 Chronicles 34:22-28), Deborah (Judges 4:1-2), Miriam (Exodus 15:20-21), and Isaiah's wife (Isaiah 8:3). Several others are mentioned in the New Testament, including Anna (Luke 2:36-68) and the daughters of Philip (Acts 21:8-9).

Consider the story of Huldah, whose prophecy takes place under the reign of Josiah, king of Judah during the seventh century BCE. Josiah desired to restore the worship of God in Jerusalem and to restore the temple. During that time, the high priest Hilkiah discovered the Book of the Law and sent it to be read to King Josiah. Upon hearing the words of the scroll, words that declare God's anger at the people's actions, Josiah was shocked and anguished. He tore his garments in distress and lament and sent his high priest and leaders to inquire of Huldah what could be done to rectify the major infraction caused by his forefathers. She responded:

> "Thus says the LORD, the God of Israel: Regarding the words that you have heard, because your heart was penitent and you humbled yourself before God when you

heard his words against this place and its inhabitants, and you have humbled yourself before me, and have torn your clothes and wept before me, I also have heard you, says the LORD. I will gather you to your ancestors and you shall be gathered to your grave in peace; your eyes shall not see all the disaster that I will bring on this place and its inhabitants" (2 Chronicles 34:26-28, NRSV).

This passage verifies that a woman's word was highly valued by the king of Judah. Her prophecies were respected; there were no inquiries regarding her gifts or her calling from God. Gender never became a part of the conversation. Huldah's role as prophet was never questioned in the text.

Other affirmations of the key role of women in God's story flow throughout the Scriptures. The Old Testament prophet Joel declared that God would pour out his Spirit upon women as well as men and they would prophesy (Joel 2:28-29). Jesus allowed women among the fellowship of his close followers (Mark 15:40-41; Luke 8:1-3), an act most teachers of his day would have viewed as scandalous. Each of the four Gospel writers reported that women were the first witnesses of the resurrection—although the male disciples dismissed their testimony. And Paul proclaims that in Christ there is no distinction between male and female; all are one in Christ Jesus (Galatians 3:28).

Gender and Power

Although patriarchal interpretations (and misinterpretations) of Scripture have shaped attitudes toward women, we need to delve deeper to understand fully the current discrimination against women in ministry. To flesh out causes for the dearth of women in the role of senior pastor, it is important to consider some underlying issues that influence a congregation's choice not to call a woman as pastor.

From a sociopolitical standpoint, power, sex, and ignorance are the major issues—rather than theology, Scripture, or gifts for ministry. When it comes to Christian character, commitment to preaching and teaching the gospel of Jesus Christ, education, experience, references, leadership abilities, and suitability for a given body of believers, the women applying for pastoral positions are usually just as qualified as—or more qualified than—their male counterparts. However, women are still far less likely to be offered such leadership roles. Often, even those who most vehemently oppose having women in church leadership remain close-lipped about the real reasons for their reluctance. But when pushed to explain, those who oppose women in the pastorate may offer the following reasons:

- A woman is not strong enough to lead.
- It's not God's will for a woman to become a pastor.
- A woman should be at home with her husband and children.
- A woman can't handle oversight of a church.
- Men will not follow a woman.

In many ways, churches have remained captive to the patriarchal character of the larger culture. Although women have made great strides in recent decades, society in the United States remains patriarchal, and women still lag behind men in top-level positions and salaries.

The complex dynamics of racism also play a role in the oppression of women of color. For some communities of color in the United States—especially the African American community—the church is one of the few places where men hold positions of power and influence. These men may be considered of nominal influence on the job or in the marketplace, but when they come to church, they are deacons, elders, bishops, or pastors. Men may be reluctant to share these leadership roles with women.

Yet often the most vocal opponents of female pastors are not men but other women. Some women view female clergy as being "out of biblical order," usurping the authority of men in the church. In his article about women pastors, Darryl Izzard quotes one female reader who believes men should lead in both home and church:

> I am a woman. I have been happily married to a God-fearing man for twenty-two years, and it has been the best of my life. I see my husband as the head of the household. He is head Elder in our local church. He is also a lay Pastor. I would never dream of usurping his authority in the home or the church. The marriage in our home and in the church works because we live the Biblical principles of a husband and a wife. I honor him as head of the home, and he honors me as his helpmate, companion, and friend.[2]

What a tragedy that such thinking is still an issue in the twenty-first century! Yet many women share this belief that female pastors are in violation of God's ordained structure for the family and the church. In the minds of these individuals, the clergywoman's assertion that God has called her to lead a congregation seems heretical. And those who operate under this assumption can be quite difficult (but not impossible) to convince otherwise.

Other women are resistant to female pastors because of fears and desires of which they may not even be aware. For some women, the male pastor is the only man in their lives. He is the only man for whom they can bake a cake or a pie, relish the authoritativeness of his voice, or cherish how proud he makes them feel as he represents them in the larger community. They appreciate the male pastor as a role model for their sons, especially those young men who may not have a father figure at home. He makes them feel safe and satisfied psychologically.

Ruth Brandon Minter illuminates these issues, explaining that unconscious and unarticulated emotions related to sexuality often drive women's resistance to female pastors.[3] As an example, Minter speaks about the interactions between male pastors and older women who may be widowed or never married. Many of these women primarily have other older women as friends. The only "safe" male touch a woman in this life situation experiences may come on Sunday morning when she greets the pastor. The male pastor's warm embrace or grasp of her hand affirms and validates her womanhood. His comments about her beautiful hat or outfit may generate feelings of appreciation and a joy that someone still finds her attractive. For younger women, the male pastor may be a welcomed male confidant who can counter derogatory or hurtful comments from insensitive men. If he is attractive, personable, and fun to be with, the male pastor can fill a void for female parishioners that a woman cannot.

Despite being written nearly two decades ago, Minter's observations still hold true today. These realities are formidable and extremely difficult to overcome. To further explore what stands in the way of progress for female clergy, it is important to consider the circumstances that breed divisions among women.

Complexities of the *Imago Dei*

Imago Dei is a Latin phrase that means "image of God." It is a theological concept that asserts that we humans, both men and women, were created in the image of God (Genesis 1:27) and are therefore god-like in nature. God placed within each of us a reflection of the divine self; in other words, we have some of God's traits. God granted us dominion over the earth; therefore, we desire to lead. God breathed into us the Spirit; therefore, we are aware that we are more than what seems readily apparent. God has imprinted us with a divine sense of a purpose and a plan; therefore, we desire to become more than what our present circumstances may dictate.

Although we are not worthy of the praise due to God's holy name, we also desire praise. As Christians, we know that to walk in the Spirit means we must avoid selfishness, pride, and arrogance. However, we all desire healthy recognition, appreciation, and praise, and if we are honest, we acknowledge that desire. In an environment where honor, praise, appreciation, respect, opportunity, and unconditional love are shared appropriately, issues of jealousy and power playing should be minimal. Because of our fallen nature, some residue of sinful pride and envy may exist, but these should not dominate.

When gifts and talents are truly recognized, when opportunities to grow and rise are present, and when honor, respect, and praise are appropriately given, rivalry is negligible. Women, however, consistently have been denied access to the inherent blessings of God's endowment to humanity. When any individual or group is disrespected, underappreciated, and denied opportunities, the "crab in the bucket" mentality will thrive. A tendency to push others down in order to grab one of the few places at the top will abound. When individuals are forced to struggle and fight for any kind of recognition, when they are weary of being passed over, divisions and strife will prevail. Oppression produces strange fruit and unfortunate results. Those who have been oppressed often become that which they claim to despise.

A few women have been able to break through the stained glass ceiling to become the pastors of large churches that are financially stable and thriving. However, there is a certain lure of elitism for those who have made it into the club. Often, those who have broken through the glass ceiling neglect to help others climb through the cracks. When a struggling female minister reaches out to be mentored by a successful sister in the pastorate, her phone calls, e-mails, and cards may go unanswered. When preaching or work-shop opportunities open at the church of a successful female pas-tor, she may find it easier to offer such openings to popular male clergy or another sister who has already made it. Often, little atten-tion or effort goes to encouraging new female ministers who are climbing the ladder.

Sexism and racism have some tragic similarities. Racial minorities have been given "compliments" such as "You are so intelligent! You are not like *them*. You are different!" The impli-cation is obvious: "*You people* are usually ignorant and inca-pable, but somehow you're not like the rest." What an insult! Many persons of color have heard these words not as insults but rather as a reprieve from oppression—a welcomed affirmation, a hint of praise. Women have dealt with the same dynamics as they have reached higher levels. Out of extreme thirst for accept-ance, they drink in patronizing words such as, "You aren't like those other women; you can preach," or, "I like how feminine you are; you aren't trying to act like a man." When one is psy-chologically and emotionally hungry, it is tempting to be drawn into the illusion of acceptance and relish the thought of being a part of the upper crust.

A woman who gains one of the precious few spots on the other side of the glass ceiling is faced with a choice. She can guard her status and bask in the warmth of artificial acceptance while know-ing that true acceptance of women in ministry would open the door wider for others. Or she can reject and challenge patronizing remarks like, "We like you because you aren't always preaching about women's rights." She can seize that moment to engage the one making the remark in a different conversation. She can high-light the many reasons why women may feel compelled to speak often about their rights or preach "like a man" due to the lack of female role models in the pastorate. She can emphasize the gifts and anointing God places upon all who are called to pastor, irrespective of gender. Without condoning the overly aggressive behaviors sometimes exhibited by wounded women, the female pastor who has broken through can assist by clearing the barriers for others. She can cultivate a heightened awareness of the painful realities women face as they struggle to accept and pursue their God-given calling.

For some women pastors the feelings of superiority and the sweet taste of acceptance can seem far more attractive than staying in the trenches and fighting so others can share the stage. After all, martyrs die—and who wants to make that kind of sacrifice? Too often, women do more to stand in the way of progress and suppress one another's goals and accomplishments than does any man.

Apostle Dr. Mamie J. Harris Smith reflected on the struggles some women have in supporting other women:

> I think out of ignorance some women come against women pastors. Some have the mindset that women are not supposed to preach. Some women do not respect women pastors the same way they respect a man. They want you to be their "girlfriend." If you are anointed, they feel threatened by you. They are afraid that you may come back and rise above them.
>
> I try to make a platform for others. That's what trailblazers do. You have to be secure in yourself. If you can't support others you have to understand why. It is because of unmet needs, unresolved issues, and unhealed hurts.[4]

Pastor Marilyn Parker-Jeffries, founder of New Creation Baptist Church in Lorain, Ohio, provided the following insights when asked to highlight some of the common challenges and opportunities that come with church leadership:

One of the challenges for me is balancing the church pastorate with the community pastorate. In terms of being a leader in the community, which is how African American pastors are viewed, some of the demands that get placed on our time for community-related events and ministry make it difficult to balance the need to serve in the local congregation. There are only so many boards on which you can serve or events for which you can do the invocation.

Another challenge is learning to erect boundaries for myself as a pastor. I have found it is really true that parishioners think they can call you any time even though the bulletin states my office hours. In a small church, office hours are an anomaly. They don't really exist.

Because we are a minority, seeking to find like-minded sisters in ministry can be difficult. The cattiness and the jealousy can create isolation. In response, I think we can try to get a cross section of women pastors together with each one sharing her gifts. Hopefully, we can break down misconceptions that we might have about one another simply because we don't know one another.

Pastor Parker-Jeffries believes traditionalism is one of the primary obstacles preventing women from being called to a senior pastorate. She explains:

The leading pastorate role has traditionally been seen as a male role. We've allowed that view to morph into behaviors and mindsets that make it difficult for us to consider looking beyond our tradition. We've allowed ourselves to become entrenched in certain ways of thinking without understanding why that's the way it is and always has been.

She notes that these traditional views are often rooted in faulty understandings of the Scriptures:

> Dr. Marvin McMickle, the new president of Colgate-Rochester Divinity School, said poor exegesis has caused much of the problem. That's the bottom line. Out of the pulpits we've had poor exegesis. That has been the major barrier that has prevented women from assuming their rightful place in the kingdom. I had to wrestle when I heard God call me because I'd never been taught it was right for women to preach. I experienced a dual wrestling match between the call to preach (which was mind-boggling in itself) and what that meant for me as a woman, something that I'd never seen before. That struggle precipitated the development of a panic disorder within me. I was a wreck.

How many other women have been confronted with this same struggle, hearing God's call while trying to reconcile that calling with their traditions? However, women as well as a growing number of men have pushed through this traditionalism driven by poor exegesis and have chosen rather to honor the voice of God.

Pastor Parker-Jeffries also shares an experience that stresses the importance of women from different Christian traditions breaking down barriers and getting to know one another:

> Years ago, when I became a part of a newly planted ministry, I was asked to serve on the ministry team with several other women. We came from various denominations—Baptist, Apostolic, Holiness. The "Holiness" women particularly intimidated me. They just seemed, so, "holy"—filled with the Holy Ghost—and they were "tongue talking," anointed women of God. I was sooo intimidated by

them. How was I going to minister alongside these holy women? So I made the decision to just open up and tell them how I felt—intimidated! To my surprise, they embraced me with love and told me how they had heard about my anointing and gifts, and that they were intimidated by me!

After we shared openly with one another, we got past our preconceived notions and worked together beautifully. A spirit of authenticity broke down the barriers between us.[5]

Ageism

Many women seeking a lead pastoral role are also forced to contend with another obstacle: ageism, or discrimination based on a person's age. I witnessed a service a few years ago in which three individuals were being ordained. As the congregation prayed, sang songs, and heard congratulatory remarks, one could not help but notice something striking about the three candidates. At the front of the church stood two young men, probably in their thirties, and one distinguished older woman, in her mid-sixties. "I finally made it!" she testified.

Although the ordination was a joyous occasion, a tinge of sadness was in the air. At an age when most people prepare to retire, this woman was just starting in ordained ministry. One can imagine the number of years she toiled, prayed, struggled, and waited for someone to say, "Yes, I will ordain you." Surely her trust is in the Lord, for if human standards were the sole determining factor in her journey toward the ministry, her ordination was merely a symbolic gesture. If it were up to human beings alone, it is unlikely that any doors to the pastorate would open for her. With God, however, all things are possible!

As we have noted earlier, most women who enter the pastorate do so later in life. But age also has a direct bearing upon the opportunities available to them. Many clergywomen face discrimination due to both gender and age (and for minorities, it can be gender, age, and race). A 2009 study by the Barna Group found that the median age of female pastors has risen during the previous ten years, from fifty years of age to fifty-five. Although the median age of male senior pastors is younger, it too has risen—from age forty-eight to fifty-two.[6]

Many of the women entering the pastorate in their forties, fifties, and sixties might well have pursued pastoral ministry at a younger age if the church had been more supportive of this calling for women. In *Clergy Women: An Uphill Calling*, Barbara Brown Zikmund, Adair T. Lummis, and Patricia M. Y. Chang share the results of their survey of female clergy. About one-third of the clergywomen in their study decided to become ordained at the age of thirty or older—three times the number of men who made this same decision after age thirty. They also found that in "more theologically conservative Spirit-centered denominations," five times as many women as men first seriously considered becoming clergy at age thirty or older.[7] Reflecting on these statistics, the authors state:

> God may call an individual, but if family, church and society withhold support, it is hard for people to believe that this is what God really intends them to do with their lives. In many of the denominations in our study, women professing a call from God to enter the ordained ministry were not well received. They were scorned, told that they were overstepping their female role, and considered guilty of lying or pathetic self-delusion when they shared such an idea. This made it very difficult for many women to tell anyone what they thought God was calling them

to do, especially denominational officials serving as gate-keepers to the ordination process.[8]

Because many women enter the ministry at an older age and many churches are reluctant to call older individuals to a first pastorate, age became another barrier facing many women who pursue pastoral ministry. However, God still has the last say!

Rev. Julia Moses is a senior clergywoman who served as associate minister at Covenant Baptist Church in Wickliffe, Ohio, for six years. With wisdom, vibrancy, and charisma, Rev. Moses is determined to pursue her calling despite ageism. In this interview, you can hear courage and perseverance against the odds. For her, age truly is just a number.

CS: How old were you when you entered seminary?

JM: I was in my sixties.

CS: How did you feel as an older student?

JM: At first, I wondered how I was going to get along with these younger students who were full of energy and bright. Initially, after looking at the members of the class and seeing how they responded so quickly to answering the questions, I began to question whether or not I could survive! So after my first encounter, I went home and got on my knees and said, "Lord, are you sure that I am supposed to be in seminary at this age? There is no one there who resembles me in terms of my hair and my appearance!" However, when I returned to class several days later, I was greeted very warmly by two students, a male and a female, who asked me if I wanted to study with them. I was a little reluctant, but I said, "Yes, I'll sit in with you!" As we talked about our books and homework assignments, they told me that they would help me with whatever I needed. They were two angels that God sent my way.

CS: You have shared openly that you desire to become a senior pastor. What comments have you received from mentors regarding your desire at this stage of your life?

JM: Upon first revealing my desire to be a senior pastor, it was met with unanticipated negativity. The question was asked, "Don't you think you are too old for that?" I had not considered my age because I have been and continue to be in reasonably good health. I have a lot of stamina, and I believe it is what God wants me to do. Also, I have witnessed my male counterparts who were my age and older being called and serving as interims or senior pastors. One of my well-respected mentors said to me, "You are in your sixties now. You certainly don't want to be seventy years old dragging up and down to a pulpit!"

CS: How did those remarks and the perception of you being too old affect your desire and fervor to pursue that calling?

JM: Because of my respect for spiritual leadership, I withdrew. I said to myself that this must not be where the Lord wants me to be. I did not openly talk about my heart's desire again for approximately three years.

CS: What reopened that conversation for you?

JM: The conversation was reopened by the prompting of the Holy Spirit, the depth of my desire to pastor, and the goals and the mission that I have for the pastoral ministry. I asked myself the question, "Am I going to listen to what God is telling me or am I going to listen to the voices of men and women who would look at me as if I had two heads?" I made the decision to follow the Lord. I believe my call is to become a senior pastor. It is my hope that people will look past my age, and see the Christ in me, and what I have to offer. I know that I would not likely be a senior pastor for a long period of time. However, that further adds to my desire to train and groom others in the ministry—others I could continue to mentor, men and women.[9]

Ageism, dysfunctional frameworks, insecurities, traditionalism, and misinterpretation of Scripture have all served as hindrances to the opening of doors for women in ministry. One female survey respondent said this when asked why some women pastors might struggle to support other women in ministry:

> I think women pastors support other women *ministers.* However, I think it is mixed concerning women pastors supporting other women *pastors.* So many are just lone rangers, not grooming anybody else—not reaching out to other clergywomen who are pastors. Sometimes we are isolated depending upon where we pastor. We are inundated because we are mothers or take care of our elderly parents. Our time is so constrained so we fail to make it a priority. We should, but we don't do it.
>
> Also, insecurity plays a part. When you've had to be on your own, even if you have a mentor, you have to do a lot of things yourself. The road can be rough, and you become jaded. You have to deal with your issues and insecurities before you can help others. Frequently, you have not dealt with insecurities, your issues from childhood, sometimes not even your marriage. You just push it aside and keep moving. Therefore you don't have a capacity to have a loving relationship with other pastors or people—you can't be a good friend to other people. —*Ohio*

The Power of Perception and Denial

Self-perception is powerful. We have received so many mixed messages about what it means to be a woman that we often struggle to identify and maintain a healthy self-image. Clergywomen are no different. An unhealthy self-image will thwart progress. An anonymous writer (http://answers.yahoo.com/question/index?qid=2008 1101222455AASsM1T from the *Yahoo Answers website*) shared, "People tend to live life like theater, acting with masks that read other than what they truly are." Shakespeare emphasized the need for authenticity in these famous words from *Hamlet*:

> This above all: to thine own self be true,
> And it must follow, as the night the day,
> Thou canst not then be false to any man.[10]

One would think that clergywomen, as bearers of the Truth (the Word of the holy God), would walk, live, and breathe truth as a way of being. However, due to human frailty, we also fall prey to perception and denial. When masks are worn to hide our inward and outward struggles, not only are others deceived, but ultimately we become deceived about ourselves. The fear of what others may think, the concern over how we will appear, the dread of being pushed out or locked out of certain places, and the superwoman syndrome all play a part in our tendency to deny our own struggles.

My research for this book included a survey of more than one hundred female senior pastors regarding the pressures of ministry in the local church. Each pastor was asked to respond to a series of statements by indicating whether she strongly agreed, moderately agreed, moderately disagreed, or strongly disagreed.

In response to the statement, "I find myself wearing many hats to handle the day-to-day operation of the church," an overwhelming 83 percent indicated that they strongly or moderately agreed. Of course, "wearing many hats" means different things to different people—but the image definitely suggests a juggling act of sorts. Women tend to be multitaskers by nature. Also, because women tend to pastor smaller, struggling churches that are often financially unstable, there may be minimal human and monetary resources. Many of these pastors use their own money to fund activities, pay church bills, and support mission efforts. Often they are without associate staff or laypersons who are willing to help conduct necessary matters of church operation. Alongside the primary roles of preacher and pastoral caregiver, a woman pastor may find herself expected to conduct most church meetings, answer phones, develop and print bulletins, visit the sick—and raise the dead! And all this is in addition to the many and various important roles she may play outside of the church—daughter, wife, mother, sister, and friend—plus her involvement in other community activities and associations.

Indeed, most women pastors do wear many hats and parcel energy into many and varied areas of service. That is why it is simultaneously interesting and disconcerting that the majority of women in the survey *disagreed* with the following statement: "I frequently feel frustrated because of the lack of resources and finances to carry on the ministry of the church." More than half of the clergywomen surveyed (56%) disagreed with this statement. More than half of the pastors in the survey would not admit to frustration in the midst of minimal resources. Women in general—and religious women in particular—have been taught to accept what is available and make do. Although the desire to break through the glass ceiling may be present, the belief that a pastor deserves to have more may feel antithetical to godliness. Therefore, she grins and bears her difficult circumstances. To cover her pain, she wears a mask.

Many give the impression that all is well, that they are doing fine, and that nothing is falling through the cracks (including their physical, mental, and spiritual health) because they believe it is absolutely necessary to keep the ball rolling at any expense. But continuing to wear the mask, continuing to pretend to be unaffected by the intense pressures of minimal resources, continuing to behave as if it's all good is not just denial; it can also be deadly!

Why do so many clergywomen wear the mask? Perhaps it is because we fear how others will perceive us if we admit that all is not well. Maybe we want to avoid appearing weak or inadequate. If we admit our struggles, we are afraid someone will say, "See? Pastoring is a man's job, and a woman can't handle it." We want to prove that women are good enough, strong enough, and smart enough to get the job done. So we may buy into the lie that the false perceptions and negative opinions of others somehow control our destiny. But by continuing to wear a mask, we prevent ourselves from receiving the help that may be available; thus, we remain stuck in downward spiraling environments.

God declared that it is not good that one should be alone (Genesis 2:18). Although these words from Scripture were spoken in the context of God's creating a helpmate for Adam, they also speak to the need of every human being to live in community. When clergywomen continue to wear masks and deny their struggles, frustrations, pain, and need for help, they miss opportunities for God to bring support, assistance, and healing into their lives.

The superwoman image also sets a bad example for the people of God. The "do it all yourself" mentality is dysfunctional. God provides support systems in human form. If clergywomen are to break through the glass ceiling and move beyond the broken fragments on the other side, they will need to remove the mask of denial and be honest with themselves and others.

Low Expectations

Commonly, women are reluctant to take practical steps toward advancement. In *Women Don't Ask: Negotiation and the Gender Divide*, Linda Babcock and Sara Laschever contend that women tend to have low expectations for themselves and often lack knowledge of their true worth. The authors have found that many women are grateful to be offered a job, so they are willing accept whatever salary is offered rather than negotiating. They also suggest that women often do not know the market value of their work. Women report salary expectations that are between 3 and 32 percent lower than the expectations of men for the same jobs. On average, men expect to earn 13 percent more than women during their first year of full-time work, and 32 percent more at the peak of their careers.[11]

Although the data reflect the expectations of women in the secular realm, clergywomen frequently make the same mistakes. And, in the case of clergy, personal theologies may further cloud the issue. A clergywoman may think that negotiating for a higher salary or a higher-level position is haughty or materialistic. She may believe that being willing to accept a low-paying, low-benefit, high-responsibility pastoral position at a struggling congregation is a way of honoring God—and in some cases, this may be true. But she may not be aware that historical and societal influences are at play in her way of thinking.

Low expectations create a psychological and emotional ceiling that prevents women from reaching the heights they might otherwise achieve. In order for clergywomen to break through the stained glass ceiling, we must be willing to expand our thinking, expect higher and better for ourselves, and know that God is not displeased by our desire to rise. We must understand that God's power in our lives and ministries will not diminish if we gain entrance to higher levels or positions, because it is God who lifts us up (Psalm 75:6-7).

As discouraging as the stories and statistics in this chapter may be, we must explore the realities of the struggle if we would develop strategies to break through the barriers. Just as women travail in labor to bring forth the beauty of new life, so women in ministry must bear down and push until a new reality is birthed.

When you are tempted to give up, consider the words of Isaac Watts in his great hymn:

> Must I be carried to the skies
> on flowery beds of ease,
> while others fought to win the prize,
> and sailed through bloody seas?
>
> Are there no foes for me to face?
> Must I not stem the flood?
> Is this vile world a friend to grace,
> to help me on to God?
>
> Sure I must fight, if I would reign;
> increase my courage, Lord.
> I'll bear the toil, endure the pain,
> supported by thy word.[12]

"Therefore, my beloved, be steadfast, immovable, always excelling in the work of the Lord, because you know that in the Lord your labor is not in vain" (1 Corinthians 15:58, NRSV).

Notes

1. Bonnidell Clouse and Robert G. Clouse, eds., *Women in Ministry: Four Views* (Downers Grove, IL: InterVarsity Press, 1989); Denvis O. Earls, *Daughters of God: Southern Baptist Women in the Pulpit: Heresy vs. the Call to Preach* (Frederick, MD: PublishAmerica, 2006).

2. Darryl Izzard, "*Gospel Today* Returns with a Cover Featuring Dynamic Women Pastors," GospelToday.com, January 9, 2011, http://mygospeltoday.com/?p=2444 (accessed November 21, 2012).

3. Ruth Brandon Minter, "Hidden Dynamics Block Women's Access to Pulpits," *Christian Century*, August 29–September 5, 1994, 805.

4. Christine A. Smith, interview with Mamie J. Harris Smith, Griffin, Georgia, October 2011.

5. Christine A. Smith, interview with Marilyn Parker-Jeffries, Cleveland, Ohio, December 2011.

6. The Barna Group, "Number of Female Senior Pastors in Protestant Churches Doubles in Past Decade," http://www.barna .org/barna-update/article/17-leadership/304-number-of-female-senior-pastors-in-protestant-churches-doubles-in-past-decade (accessed November 21, 2012).

7. Barbara Brown Zikmund, Adair T. Lummis, and Patricia M. Y. Chang, *Clergy Women: An Uphill Calling* (Louisville: Westminster John Knox, 1998), 98.

8. Zikmund, Lummis, and Chang, *Clergy Women*, 98.

9. Christine A. Smith, interview with Julia Moses, Cleveland, Ohio, July 2012.

10. William Shakespeare, *Hamlet*, act 1, scene 3, lines 78–82.

11. Linda Babcock and Sara Laschever, *Women Don't Ask: Negotiation and the Gender Divide* (Princeton: Princeton University Press, 2003); overview, "Interesting Statistics," http://www.womendontask.com/stats.html (accessed November 21, 2012).

12. Isaac Watts, "Am I a Soldier of the Cross?" (1761).

CHAPTER 4

How Shall We Get There?

Yet amid all these things we are more than conquerors and gain a surpassing victory through Him Who loved us.
(Romans 8:37, Amplified Bible)

When considering getting there, the essential questions are: What guidance can women senior pastors give to sister clergy who feel called to become pastors but lack direction and opportunity? What specific equipment is important to have on the path to becoming a senior pastor? What words of encouragement and insight can we share with those who have already become senior pastors but are seeking encouragement, suggestions for enhancing their ministries, or additional pastoral opportunities?

This chapter discusses some of the experiences and perceptions of senior female pastors as they journeyed through the doors that have begun to open for women. While each pastor's journey is different, several factors emerge as common in their successes: education, getting connected and networking, being patient yet persistent, being open to serving in a variety of venues, and being creative. For female clergy endeavoring to be as successful, I recommend that they embrace these key concepts.

Get Educated

In this book's survey of female senior pastors from freewill denominations, 71.4 percent have a master's degree in some area of pastoral preparation (MDiv, MAR, MTh, MA) and 21.4 percent have a doctoral degree. These numbers suggest that earning a degree beyond the bachelor's level is critical. Many denominations, such as American Baptist Churches USA, United Church of Christ, and Disciples of Christ, strongly urge congregations to call clergy who have at least a master's degree in religious studies. While freewill congregations may call whomever they choose, excellent credentials can help to move an application closer to the top of the pile.

According to a *CBS Evening News* report, women are strengthening their credentials. "Since 1972 the number of males enrolled in seminary has fallen 25 percent. But over the same time frame female enrollment has increased from 5 percent to 31 percent."[1] Although women are enrolling in seminary at greater numbers than males, they still lag significantly in being called to pastorates. The saying "You must be twice as good to get half as much" is not an overstatement in the case of women seeking to become senior pastors.

As preparation for the pastorate, women may have many questions regarding the kind of higher degree to pursue. Questions regarding school selection, options for financial assistance, and school location may abound. The following section provides some helpful hints.

Description of Theological Degrees

The following information about theological degrees was adapted from the Fund for Theological Education website.[2]

Master of divinity (MDiv). The primary degree offered in theological schools is the master of divinity (MDiv), which can also be called the master of ministry (MMin) or be offered at the undergraduate levels as a bachelor of divinity (BD). The MDiv is the basic degree for parish or ordained ministry. According to the Association for Theological Schools (ATS), degrees for ministerial formation should enable students to develop in four primary areas:

■ Comprehensive and critical understanding of the local faith community;
■ Awareness of the cultural and social realities in which ministry occurs, including the faith community itself;
■ Emotional, spiritual, intellectual, and social formation for the practice of ministry;
■ Capacity to enter and effectively practice a specific form of vocational ministry.

Most MDiv programs take approximately three years to complete for full-time students.[3] MDiv students must take a broad range of classes, from the classical disciplines of theology, biblical studies, ethics, and history to practical courses in counseling, homiletics (preaching), liturgics (worship), and education. Students who plan to be ordained will also take courses required by their denomination, such as church polity, church administration, or denominational history. MDiv programs also require a field education or internship in a setting that exposes the student to the daily experience of ministry. Depending upon the school, field education requirements may be fulfilled in a parish, hospitals, nursing homes, prisons, or social service agencies. Most MDiv programs require students to share their field education experience in writing and small-group work, in order to allow students to share their experiences with other future ministers.[4]

Specialized ministerial degrees. Many schools offer religious degrees other than the MDiv to prepare individuals for ministry in specific areas of pastoral skills. Often, fewer course requirements and less time are needed to complete them. Some denominations will accept alternative degrees for credentialing purposes, though these degrees do not offer the same comprehensive preparation as the MDiv. Other degree programs may focus upon Christian ministries, Christian leadership, theological studies, and pastoral ministry. Some focus upon specific fields such as counseling, Christian or religious education, missions, spiritual formation, sacred music, and liturgics. Alternative programs may provide certificates or diplomas and take less than three years to complete.

Doctoral degrees. The most common advanced ministerial degree is the doctor of ministry (DMin).[5] This degree is designed for students with the MDiv who wish to further develop a particular skill or approach to ministry. Some schools offer a continuous MDiv to DMin program wherein students can complete both degrees in four or five years. Most DMin formats, however, require students to have extensive practical experience in ministry before starting the program. The DMin offers advanced skills and perspectives to ministers and can help to open doors of opportunity for denominational leadership at the regional and national levels.

Theological schools may also offer doctor of philosophy (PhD) and doctor of theology (ThD) degrees in a variety of fields. Students who have an interest in research, teaching, or scholarly writing are encouraged to pursue degrees at this level. At university-related institutions, the PhD may be offered through the university's graduate school rather than the theological school. In the theological and religious disciplines, completion of a master's degree is generally preferred before applying to doctoral programs, though this may not be required in every program.

Denominational Requirements and Choosing a School
When selecting a school, clergy should first familiarize themselves with their denomination's requirements for pastoral positions. Some denominations require their ministers to complete part or

all of a master's program before being called to a position as a senior pastor. Some denominations require that clergy attend specific schools within their denominational body. Those denominations maintain a list of schools that they deem acceptable for ministry preparation.

Accreditation. A critical aspect of selecting a school should be whether or not the school has proper accreditation. Many students have wasted precious time and resources paying for an online seminary degree or attending a local Bible college only to discover that the program did not have the appropriate credentials. In order to gain accreditation an institution must go through a rigorous process wherein it is evaluated by an external organization for educational quality and effectiveness. For graduate theological education, the Commission on Accrediting of the Association of Theological Schools serves as this agency. To be accredited, a school must go through an initial review that examines a wide variety of factors, including library holdings, faculty quality, and financial stability. The ATS commissioners repeat this process on a regular basis to make sure that each of its schools maintains an acceptable level of academic quality.[6]

Differences in school names. Graduate-level religious schools have different titles, such as seminary, divinity school, or school of theology. In addition to these, theological schools are also called schools of religion, theological institutes, or theological consortiums. Is there any significance to the different names? Yes and no. They all have commitments to forming ministers (broadly defined) for church and society, but they are organized in different ways that have an effect on their students.

Divinity schools are almost always related to an established university and act as one academic unit among many others, such as business, education, law, and humanities. Students at university-related divinity schools usually have access to the resources of the larger university, including a full range of library holdings, faculty and courses in other fields, and facilities and services associated with the larger institution.

Seminaries are usually freestanding institutions related to a particular denomination or religious movement but independent of a college or university. This environment can be powerful for students' faith formation.

Schools of theology or religion represent a third category of theological schools. Some schools of theology and religion are closely related to universities; others are free-standing, like seminaries. Others maintain relationships with other educational institutions or communities without maintaining official ties. Still others operate in theological consortia, where a number of schools from different traditions come together to offer a unique breadth of opportunities for students.[7]

Some important questions a student should consider when choosing an institution are: Which type of institution can best serve your interests and calling? Where can you get the most flexibility as you grow into your vocation in these schools? Does the school seem to be the best fit for preparing you in what you are seeking or feel called to do?

Mission statement and statement of faith. Female clergy in particular should pay close attention to a school's mission statement and statement of faith. Schools that teach only literal interpretation of the biblical text, for example, may not be the best fit for a female pastor. Some schools have lengthy statements of faith that detail specific theological points in order to carefully define a confessional stance. Other schools deliberately have less specific statements of faith in order to encourage open-minded exploration of theological perspectives.[8]

Location and setting. A woman entering seminary, particularly if she is a wife and mother, may feel limited in her options for selecting a program due to family obligations. However, it is important to consider prayerfully the location and setting of a school. While it may be easier to attend a local seminary, the school nearby may not offer the courses or programs for particular ministries. When possible, women should prayerfully and carefully explore all options suitable to a particular calling and service. Geographic location should not be the predominant factor in choosing a school.

Student body. The size of a school's student body is important. Theological schools range from very small—ten to twenty people—to very large institutions with thousands of students. You can discover significant differences among theological schools based on the size of their student bodies. Average class sizes, access to faculty, and institutional resources can be directly determined by the number of students enrolled at a school.

Across all theological schools in the United States and Canada, students under the age of thirty still represent the largest group (28 percent). However, other age groups are nearly equal to this percentage, with thirty- to thirty-nine-year-olds representing 26 percent, forty- to forty-nine-year-olds 25 percent, and those over fifty 21 percent. In the classroom, this means all students can benefit from diverse academic and professional experiences as well as intergenerational perspectives that can significantly influence theological reflection and construction.[9]

In your search, you will also note that schools vary greatly in the racial and ethnic makeup of their student bodies. On the whole, theological education is attracting a more diverse student body, but many schools are not ethnically diverse. This will affect the content and approaches to theological education, so consider this aspect when choosing a school.

Faculty. It is also important to take a close look at the faculty at a theological school. Though it takes some research, you can learn much about a school through the character of its faculty. First, look at the distribution of the faculty among the theological disciplines. In part, the faculty make-up reflects the academic priorities of the school. Next, look at the denominational or religious traditions of the faculty. A religiously homogeneous faculty may present a generally unified theology, while a more religiously diverse faculty will likely introduce a wider variety of theological commitments and assumptions. If you have the luxury of a campus visit, consider meeting with a one or two faculty members. If the admissions office cannot find a faculty member to meet with you, consider what this may mean about the general accessibility of the faculty when you are a student.[10]

In conclusion, a theological education can better position female clergy to advance toward the pastorate. Many denominations require a master of divinity degree or a comparable theological degree before ordination and placement or a call to the pastorate. Understanding the various aspects of theological schools—specialized degrees, denominational requirements, school accreditation, school mission statements and faith statements, school location and setting, student body, and faculty—can help clergywomen to select a school and degree program that matches their particular needs.

Get Connected

Now that we have explored a variety of topics regarding preparation through education, female clergy desiring to become pastors should also get connected. According to several of the pastors surveyed, one of the greatest mistakes that women make is to remain isolated. Certainly, "no woman is an island." Particularly in the freewill denominations, female clergy are still in the trailblazing phase of history. Many of the pastors surveyed were the first female called to their particular church (66.7 percent). Churches are still having first licentiates and first ordained women. As a result, women often find themselves searching for connections within clergy circles. Those circles that are most often male-dominated are not always the most welcoming places. Therefore, many women go it alone, unaware of networks and relationships that are available to them.

If her pastor has been supportive and led the church in licensing and/or ordaining her, a woman should consult the pastor about the best way to get involved. If, for some reason, the pastor has not been particularly supportive and may have licensed her for political or other reasons, she should still seek out individuals who will walk alongside her. The Lord will always provide a ram in the bush.

Most denominations have local or regional associations and regional, state, or national conventions. Female clergy desiring to get connected should become involved in one or more of these groups. They should get to know males and females within their denomination who may be able to share information about avenues and resources available. Regional executive ministers, directors, or organization presidents can be helpful in this regard. They can share information concerning national pulpit openings, scholarships for seminary, continuing education workshops, and the names of other female ministers in the region or nation. A woman pastor should also prayerfully seek out other female clergy with whom she can share common experiences, struggles, victories, questions, and answers through websites, associations, groups, and chat rooms.

One former church planter said, "Before becoming a pastor, I wish I was told that I should find female clergy friends. If I could do it over again, I would have surrounded myself with other female pastors." Her attempt to start and maintain a congregation did not last because she needed more support. If a pastor or church refuses to recognize a female's calling to the ministry, the woman should prayerfully consider her options before leaving the church, refrain from public displays of anger, disgust, or disrespect of the pastor and church leaders, and seek wise counsel from others outside of the congregation.

It is important to remember that God, not humans, holds her destiny and gave her the calling. God will provide someone to show her what to do and where to go. Some positive options include asking the Lord to order her steps and connecting with female clergy from other churches within and outside her denomination who have been licensed and ordained by their pastors or churches. In addition, determine if a local or regional representative is available to discuss changing denominations.

Isolation can produce bitterness, confusion, misplaced hostility, lack of forgiveness, and bad judgment. Without knowledge of resources, protocol, proper procedures, or technicalities, some women have left a church and instead go from church to church looking for affirmation and acceptance. However, before they can get sure footing in the ministry, they develop reputations for being difficult, unstable, demanding, and troublemakers. This reputation often causes women to be avoided and ignored. Healthy connections are essential for success.

Be Patient but Persistent

After obtaining an education and maximizing connections, female clergy with hearts set on the pastorate will need to be patient and persistent. One respondent put it succinctly: "Be prepared to wait for many years to find a church, and be prepared to work twice as hard in your training and education as a typical male will." A total of 52 percent of the female pastors surveyed reported that there were fewer than three senior female pastors in autonomous denominations in their city. Several hierarchical denominations are much further along in the process of calling women to serve as senior pastors (Presbyterian, 19 percent; Methodist, 15 percent;

Episcopalian, 12 percent; and Lutheran, 11 percent). Although those numbers are still low, they surpass, for example, the Southern Baptist denomination, which has fewer than 5 percent of females serving as senior pastors.[11] Therefore, if a female clergyperson desires to remain in a freewill denomination, she may have to wait longer to be called by a church.

Many of the pastors interviewed first served for years as associate ministers alongside another pastor. A few of the women were blessed to be positioned upon retirement of their senior pastor to become the congregation's next leader. A recently called pastor of a Church of God congregation said that she served twenty-seven years before her pastor retired and recommended her to the church. Now in her mid-fifties, she pastors a congregation of more than twelve hundred members. In this case and most others like hers, the male predecessor had to lay groundwork for the recommendation of the female minister. This subject will be discussed further in chapter 7, "What Will We Need to Press On?"

It would be wonderful if such examples served as the common process. However, fathers recommending daughters in the pastorate are the exceptions and not the rule. Patience alone, therefore, will not always work. One must have persistence. Becoming a senior pastor is unlike applying for any other position. One should be absolutely certain that God has placed the call, the irresistible urge to preach, teach, and shepherd God's people. Rev. Dr. Mamie Oliver, pastor of the Mountainview Community Fellowship Church in Boise, Idaho, advises:

> Follow the Lord's leading and pray a lot. Be sure that's what the Lord wants you to do. Becoming a senior pastor may not be the most important thing in ministry. God may have you spread about before becoming a pastor. Sometimes you need to "pay your dues" in other levels of

ministry. They need to work in other levels of ministry before seeking to become a senior pastor. I think that is preparation for senior pastor work. Going to school is not enough. It is just one of the things.[12]

One survey respondent cautioned,

Be completely certain that the call is from God—not just because you love the church and church work. Unless it is truly a call from God, the frustration is not worth it. When it is a call from God, there is still frustration—after all, you are working with people—but it fits in. Get as much student experience as you possibly can, and unless your leading is to children, youth, or music, avoid those specialties. It is too easy to be typecast and never seen as a senior pastor because all your experience is with youth. Take a unit of CPE (Clinical Pastoral Education) even if it is not required. It's difficult, but you learn a lot about yourself and how you respond to people and crisis and hopefully how to keep your stuff out of the way of God's work.
—*Pennsylvania*

Another survey respondent provided this insight:

Trust the Lord. If God has called you to the pastorate, then God will supply all you need for the pastorate, regardless of whether you are male or female, so don't focus on being a female. I was called to seminary, thinking that I would teach Hebrew and Old Testament background in the religious studies department of a state school. The Lord changed my plans as I was working on my doctorate. A male pastor encouraged me in ministry. I hadn't given much thought to it and things just opened up. Following the Lord's guidance will lead you to the ministry you are being prepared for. —*New York*

This pastor raised an important issue referenced by several other respondents: Don't make every sermon, every conversation, and every application about being a woman. I once heard Dr. Carolyn McCrary, one of my seminary professors, say, "Folks can see that you are a woman when you stand up! You don't need to keep saying it." If people sense that a woman is angry or frustrated, because her mantra is, "I don't get opportunities because I'm a woman, men treat me unfairly because I'm a woman, I can't get called to a church because I'm a woman," she will be avoided rather than invited. This is not to suggest that her feelings are unjustified. However, focusing upon unfortunate realities will not necessarily change them. Should voice be given to the inequities that obviously exist? Of course! However, a wiser approach must be taken.

Consider the following words of wisdom from an experienced woman pastor in her late fifties, having pastored for almost a decade:

> Know that you are called. If you are married, make certain that your husband is behind you 100 percent. Be patient— people change slowly. Remember God brings about change. Surround yourself with those who will support you. Find a good mentor—male or female. Realize there will be tough days, days you will feel that you are not making a difference, days you will question your call, and days you will cry. But remember this, there will also be really great days when you will feel God's anointing, and a peace and joy that passes all understanding. Don't have a chip on your shoulder. In other words, don't think that every challenge you face is due to the fact that you are a woman.

Some are and some aren't. Know how to pick your battles. Have a sense of humor. Be yourself. — *Ohio*

Pastor Marilyn Parker-Jeffries shares this word of encouragement:

One of the things that I asked the Lord in the planting of New Creation was that I not end up pastoring a church that was predominantly female.

I had a woman who was a member of the congregation, whose husband said it was fine for her to go to that church because he could see the spiritual growth in her being during the past year, but she should not expect him to come. True to his word, he visited on a couple of occasions. One Sunday he was visiting during a Pastor's Appreciation service. A male pastor was preaching the message. When the altar call was extended, he came forward and joined. I gave him the microphone and asked him was there something he wanted to say because I knew where he stood on women pastors. He shared how he was reading the text in the book of Romans and saw the Scripture where Junias was one of the apostles. He shared that on that particular day, Junias jumped off of the page. He then decided to go and research Junias. When he discovered that Junias was a woman, he got a revelation from the Holy Spirit.

When I think about how we shall get there, we have an advocate in the Holy Spirit working behind the scenes, validating us.[13]

On the road to there, women must always remember that the God who called them also provides the Holy Spirit, the ultimate advocate. Never underestimate the power of God's Holy Spirit to convict hearts and open doors. Being persistent in praying, networking, continuing to serve in other ministerial capacities, entering a Clinical Pastoral Education (CPE) program, seeking out a mentor, and prayerfully pursuing open pastorates with good recommendations will place you in the best position to become a senior pastor.

"We have an advocate in the Holy Spirit working behind the scenes, validating us."

Keep an Open Mind

Along with all of the preparation, connections, patience, and persistence, female pastors will also need to keep an open mind. Half the battle is having the flexibility to expand your thinking and ministry vision beyond your carefully crafted expectations. We all have hopes and dreams regarding our place of service. That is not wrong; however, we need to keep some blank pages in the scripts we have written for ourselves. God has some messages to write upon those pages. Not everyone will pastor a church with more than a thousand members, nor does everyone desire to do so. The reality is that women in general pastor smaller, struggling, frequently dying (until God uses the women to revive them!) congregations. Sociologists Mary Ellen Konleczny and Mark Chaves observe: "Several studies of clergywomen have shown that female-led congregations are small and have fewer economic organizational resources than congregations led by men. Women ministers most often serve as sole or senior pastors in small congregations, only rarely pastoring large congregations."[14]

Even among those denominations that more readily receive female pastors, the percentages of those leading large congregations are very low. In an article in *Christian Century* John Dart states,

One mark of acceptance for women pastors is lagging— only some 7 percent of Methodist congregations with more than 1,000 members are led by a female senior pastor. Methodist statisticians releasing this month the most recent data (from December 2007) said that 81 of the denomination's largest congregations were led by women pastors and 1,055 by male pastors. Another eight large congregations had men and women serving as co-pastors.[15]

In a 2011 article, Susan Beaumont writes about a video in which Sheryl Sanberg, the chief operating officer of Facebook, discussed reasons why such a small percentage of women make it to the top of their professions. Beaumont applies those insights to congregations:

> The pulpit in the large congregation, for better or worse, represents the top of the vocational ladder for clergy leaders. We can argue that serving a large congregation shouldn't automatically be the ultimate vocational target for clergy leaders, but in many ways it is. And I think that we'd all agree that there are too few women leading our largest congregations.
>
> I am regularly asked to speak at gatherings of senior clergy leaders from large congregations. There are still remarkably few women in the room. I've also noticed that the women who are present are seldom as vocal as their male counterparts.[16]

Sandberg challenges women to sit at the table and "keep their hands up" as a metaphorical way to show a need for a stronger female leadership presence. She also discusses the studies that have been done on the relationship between success and likability in leadership. The correlation between likability and success for men is very strong. For women, by contrast, success and likability are negatively correlated in our culture. To illustrate this point, one clergywoman who pastors a large (1,500+) multicultural congregation said, "When my male predecessor required staff to be responsible and accountable, he was labeled a strong leader. When I do the same, I am labeled a b-!"

Women who obtain a senior pastorate at a large congregation have to learn the fine art of balancing likeability, respect, success, and their own well-being. They must recognize the historical and cultural factors driving congregational responses to their leadership and carefully discern the difference between sexism and constructive criticism. In any congregation, the desire to be liked must not overshadow the necessity to lead responsibly and with the Holy Spirit's guidance.

In the ABCUSA Female Pastor survey, 42.3 percent of respondents pastor churches with between fifty and one hundred members. In addition, 31 percent serve as pastor to churches with fewer than fifty members. These numbers are consistent with national statistics, referenced earlier from the Barna Group studies. Females desiring to pastor freewill congregations should be open to pastoring a small church. Other possibilities exist, but being open to what is currently most prevalent will provide opportunities. If circumstances permit, be open to moving to another geographical location. Flexibility with regard to location may provide greater options for females seeking to become senior pastors. Female clergy should also be open to pastoring churches of another culture or denomination. Minority female pastors, for example, may find more acceptances from historically European mainline congregations (e.g., American Baptist, United Church of Christ, Disciples of Christ) than more traditional African American or Southern Baptist churches.

Many small congregations were once thriving, mainline, and financially stable churches. Now, however, due to changing demographics, deaths, and lifestyle transitions, their numbers have decreased dramatically, and they find themselves on the brink of closure. Unable to attract male pastors, who most frequently command a higher-level salary, they turn to female pastors. Although it is a disturbing reality that females tend to be relegated to small, dying churches, many female pastors who have accepted these calls have nurtured, developed, strengthened, and built phenomenal ministries. They, along with their congregations, have found great fulfillment, empowerment, energy, and spiritual renewal.

A survey respondent from Ohio shared this advice:

> Do I wish that we had greater financial resources and a few more hands to carry on the work of the church?— YES! However, the opportunity to know every member's name, work closely with families, experience the intimacy of a small group, and follow a child from birth to college far surpasses looking into a sea of faces each week and only knowing a small percentage of the people I serve. Ministry is done one soul at a time. The small church can and does great work for the kingdom of God! —*Ohio*

Pastors of smaller churches must be creative. Rev. Dr. Debora Jackson, former senior pastor of First Baptist Church in Needham, Massachusetts, and recently elected the executive director of the National Ministers Council, ABCUSA, describes her approach to community outreach:

> We're offering a free movie night and dinner on Friday, showing *The Help* for adults and *Puss and Boots* for kids. We purposely extended invitations to one hundred people that we don't normally reach out to—people who attend AA meetings in the church, families in the child care center and nursery school that operate in the

church, people who come to a feeding program that we help to sponsor each week. We've just purchased door hangers, and I've got a group of people who want to go door to door and hang information about the church. The word that God gave me was that I need to be "Poised for the Promised Land."[17]

Later chapters of this book will address the issue of what it will take to cultivate an atmosphere of acceptance for female senior pastors in larger congregations. Certainly, some women are called to serve smaller congregations. All are not. While one may not desire to remain at a small church, great lessons, skills, experiences, and wisdom can be gained from beginning one's pastoral ministry in a small church.

A female pastor should find out if her denomination has a central office that provides referrals. Several denominations such as The Disciples of Christ, United Church of Christ, and the American Baptist Churches USA have a process to connect potential pastors with congregations seeking to fill their pulpits. For example, ABCUSA uses the American Baptist Profile System (ABPS). Licensed and ordained clergy affiliated with an American Baptist church can fill out a personal profile that provides information about references, education, experience, and preferences for ministry venue. The central office matches clergy profiles to churches seeking potential candidates with like characteristics. Having your profile in the system gives you the opportunity to be reviewed by as many churches as your characteristics and qualifications match.

Once it is determined that the desired denomination provides the needed service, it is advisable to speak with the church pastor (if supportive) and an area or executive minister for guidance and references. Obtain the necessary forms and any additional references needed, and complete and submit them as soon as possible, remembering the profile may be the only opportunity to be introduced to a potential pulpit committee. Therefore, the profile should represent the best of what the pastor has to offer regarding her life experience, education, ministerial preparation, references, and Christian witness.

Advice for Women in the Pastorate

To this point, information has been geared toward female clergy desiring to become pastors. There is also a wealth of advice for those who already have crossed that threshold but are looking for encouragement, resources, and support. What advice can we share with one another? What insights have we as individual pastors gained that could benefit other sisters in the ministry? What bridges have we crossed that another pastor may be stepping upon as we speak? To help answer these questions, I asked a number of female pastors several open-ended questions. The following are words of advice that respondents would give women who become pastors.

> Always make sure you put your own oxygen mask on first. If you don't take care of yourself, you're not going to be much help to anyone else. — *Washington*

> Find female pastors you can trust and become friends. —*Maryland*

> Know that you are called! Validation from God must be enough. Don't take it personally when others criticize or condemn you for being a woman pastor. Stay in your lane! Build your ministry with men and women who are gifted and called. Of course, use discernment but know that you cannot build a ministry alone. — *Ohio*

Don't lose your femininity! God knew you were a woman when he called you. —*Ohio*

Do not be surprised when conflict is exhibited in the church. Be wise as serpents and innocent as doves. When sexism does emerge, recognize it and love your enemies. Do not depend on church members to like you, but keep your sense of God's love for you fully nourished in your spirit. Pray constantly. You must be twice as good as a man to be accepted in leadership. —*Massachusetts*

Take the time to get to know your congregants and the history of the congregation before attempting change. This would hold true for all who would become senior pastors, not just for women. Find a collegial group of men and women where you can hear and be heard. Learn from the experiences of others and don't hesitate to "share" forward. —*Washington*

Rev. Dr. Wilma R. Johnson is the senior pastor of the New Prospect Missionary Baptist Church in Detroit, Michigan (see chapter 2, "Where Shall We Go?"). Dr. Johnson was the first female senior pastor to be elected as a member of the Council of Baptist Pastors of Detroit and Vicinity, Inc. When asked about the keys to her success, she repeatedly replied, "Teach, preach, love, and pray." In *Giving Away My Joy*, Dr. Johnson expands upon her views of why her congregation has experienced such phenomenal growth. She gives six recommendations related to what she calls the "psalmist model" of pastoral leadership:

> *Words are powerful. I always greet them with the words, "Good morning, my family!"* She embraces her church family with these sentiments.

I earnestly pray for my entire church family, within the worship service and outside. Prayer produces and sustains joy.

A powerful worship experience is critical. When worship is powerful and meaningful, it causes joy to break forth, freeing people to praise God through their own style of expression, praying, crying, shouting, dancing, or walking around the church.

Friendship increases joy. She encourages her church members to fellowship with one another during meals after worship, midweek services, and church family gatherings such as picnics and celebrations.

Giving and gratitude encourages joy. She leads in the example of giving.

I purposefully try to choose men and women who have my heart and spirit and who will share my joy in a manner in which they will touch the lives of our church family.[18]

Dr. Johnson's model suggests that joy draws people. For her, giving away joy is essential for Christian discipleship, evangelism, church growth, and development.

Rev. Portia Wills Lee, founding pastor of Trinity Tabernacle Baptist Church in Mableton, Georgia, provided profound words to those hoping to become pastors as well as to those who are currently serving in the pastorate but may be discouraged:

> To those hoping to become pastors, I would say to remain teachable. Always know that there are people who are willing to assist you. So many sisters are just not teachable. It's as if they feel that they don't have to learn from the experiences of those who have gone before them. They should understand that there is a process and things are not going to be handed to you.

Be willing to learn from anyone in the church. It does not have to be from persons with a formal degree from a seminary. See value in everyone. Have respect for everyone. It will create a greater sense of respect from the people. They will love you and set you apart from those who are standoffish.

Don't be afraid to go to small churches where you can get some experience. You need to be with someone who will let you walk with them so that you can see the day-to-day life of a pastor. Some would rather go to larger churches, but often they are limited to sitting in the pews. They limit themselves so that they can say they belong to a large church.

Spiritual overflow cannot come until we, like the olive that gives oil, are crushed. In order for God to have us where he wants us to be, there are seasons of crushing in our lives. Pastor Wills Lee has these words for those who have already become senior pastors but are seeking encouragement, suggestions for enhancing their ministries, or additional pastoral opportunities:

Often we want to reap the work of the harvest quickly, and that just does not always happen. The words that encourage me are "they that wait upon the LORD shall renew their strength" (Isaiah 40:31, KJV). There are valley situations that you may have to go through, but the Lord will be with you. Sometimes you have to sit and wait. It's not easy waiting, and it's not easy waiting for the Lord when you are going through painful situations. Sometimes God wants to move us, and sometimes he wants us to wait. Paul's words that we will reap the harvest if we do not grow weary in well doing (Galatians 6:9) are encouraging to me. We have to learn not to measure ourselves by what it looks like to someone else. When we do so, we begin to feel inferior, insecure. Everyone was not called to pastor a large church.

If we learn to become content wherever God has us, and make the most of whatever God has blessed us with and keep our eyes on pleasing God, and keep our eyes on Jesus, it will help us to stay in peace. People tend to make everything about size. It's so easy to get caught up in "God is not pleased with me" because the church is not growing. But if you can focus upon how God is using you in the lives of people it will make it so much more palatable to be where you are.[19]

Spiritual overflow cannot come until we, like the olive that gives oil, are crushed. In order for God to have us where he wants us to be, there are seasons of crushing in our lives.

Rev. Dr. Robin E. Hedgeman, senior pastor of the Bethany Christian Church, Disciples of Christ, in Cleveland, Ohio, has these words for women pastors:

Find a place that's healthy and serve faithfully with the pastor and the leaders and the membership. Be prayerful and wait for God to open the door—not for man to open the door because often that will be with strings attached. Those that God calls, he will prepare a place for them to serve. Be open to the opportunities that God places before you. Often we miss out on the places of preparation. God opens some doors and provides some places for us to serve that are places of preparation for greater blessing that he has in store. But we are always looking for the greater and think that the smaller is insignificant. We have to crawl before we walk. The smaller opportunities are venues for greater blessings. If you are faithful over a few things he'll make you ruler over many, the Word says.

For those who are already pastoring but need encouragement and direction, Dr. Hedgeman added:

Habakkuk says, "write the vision, make it plain and run with it—it shall not lie" (Habakkuk 2:2 [paraphrased]). Have a vision for your ministry. Keep the vision before you and the people. Continue to clarify the vision and let the vision give you your marching orders. When I keep my eyes focused on the vision that God gave me instead of the people, then it gives me some encouragement to keep running. But when I keep my eyes on the people, then I have my eyes set on sights that will let me down.

I believe that there are two things that you need to have a conviction about. You must know that God called you. Second, you must know that God called you to the place where you are currently serving. If you know he called and you know he has called you where you are serving, be faithful where he has called you to serve until he opens another door for you. Everybody—whether you start a church, come after a long-term pastor, are in places that had some short term pastorates, or are a diverse church—everybody—has some difficulties on the journey. I think we ought to take our difficulties to our prayer closets, find a few faithful folks who will give you good biblical counsel and guidance, and stay the course. Be sure he called you where you are because he calls us to places and from places.[20]

All of the pastors interviewed agreed that as women travel the road to become senior pastors, they must walk by faith, and not by sight. Even once that goal is reached, the faith walk continues.

Be Effective When Resources Are Limited

Often female pastors of smaller congregations have the difficult task of wearing numerous hats to get the job done. A total of 83 percent of female pastors surveyed either strongly agreed, moderately agreed, or agreed with the statement "I find myself wearing many hats to handle the day-to-day operation of the church." One of the many challenges that pastors of smaller congregations face is the lack of individuals who help to carry on basic church ministry, including Christian education (teaching church school, Bible study, Vacation Bible School), care for the building (a buildings and grounds board), and community service. Many of the respondents are pastoring churches where the average age of a congregant is fifty-six years old (44 percent of respondents). Many reported that their churches do not have a healthy cross section of members in all age groups.

Interestingly, while some of the churches have endowments and are able to support national and international missions financially, they struggle to minister to the communities in which they dwell. Frequently, when churches find themselves in this situation, pastors struggle to help laity gain the faith and hope to serve their immediate geographical areas. As a result, the churches close their doors, sell their facilities, and divide their assets among other ministries. What can a pastor in this predicament do? What have some of the sisters in this situation done? Understanding what resources are available is imperative.

When resources are limited, creativity can thrive. The phrase "necessity is the mother of invention" speaks volumes! Sometimes, in order to get the congregation to believe that they yet have gifts, talents, and vision despite their individual ages, a pastor has to prime the pump. She may have to bring in resources from other churches that are willing to partner with her until she is able to build faith, confidence, and hope in a church that has experienced years of dearth. Partnering with other churches to have Vacation Bible School, requesting volunteers from other churches to help a small group within a church to make and serve community lunches, or inviting area choirs in to hold a concert to raise funds for a special cause are all examples of partnerships that small churches have created in order to serve their communities. When pastors work together in this way, it surprises congregants to see that ministry projects are still possible, even with a small, aging congregation. Female pastors seeking to revive their congregations should prayerfully consider reaching out to colleagues in their area to see if they would be willing to share teachers, carpenters, or musicians once or twice a month.

Some churches have what could be characterized as a stone soup mentality. In the legend of "Stone Soup,"[21] a stranger comes to a village that had been hit hard by a famine. Very hungry, he goes from place to place asking questions, giving residents the impression that he plans to stay for the night. He was told to move on, since there was not a morsel of food in the entire place. Being a clever soul, the stranger replied that he had everything he needed. He pulled out an iron cauldron from his wagon, filled it with water, and built a fire under the pot. Then, with much fanfare, he took an ordinary stone from a velvet bag, plopped it in the water, and began to loudly talk about how delicious his stone soup would be. As he licked his fingers and sniffed the broth, neighbors soon became curious about the seemingly delicious dish.

The stranger loudly proclaimed, "I do like a tasty stone soup. Of course, stone soup with cabbage, now that would be hard to beat!" Suddenly, a villager appeared, sheepishly holding a cabbage he'd "found." He added it to the pot. The stranger praised the man and spoke great things about the soup. But then he declared, "You know, I once had stone soup with cabbage and a bit of salt beef as well, and it was fit for a king!" Soon the village butcher appeared with some salt beef and plopped it into the pot. Again, the stranger talked about how delicious the stone soup was, but it would be even tastier with other vegetables. One by one, the villagers came and added their goods to the pot, and soon a delicious "stone" vegetable beef soup was prepared—enough for the entire village. The moral of the story is that by working together, with everyone contributing what they can, great things can be accomplished and all will be blessed.

An African proverb agrees with this principle "Many hands make work light." In a sense, churches that have been in a famine state, without a pastor for years, interims coming and going, Sunday after Sunday a different preacher, members dying, youth almost nonexistent, may believe that they have nothing left to give. They have enough tenacity to call a pastor, but when the pastor arrives, she is expected to single-handedly move heaven and earth to pump new life into the church. Even if the church has a few individuals from younger age groups, they have been in the "we can't do because we don't have" mode for so long that they become disengaged and even defiant. Members can even wait to see what the pastor is going to do to create the meal for the church. They want new programs, but no one steps up to provide human hands to run the programs. They desire special activities, but when they are planned, no one shows up, even if they provided the suggestions for the activity. They want the youth department to grow and have youth activities, but they are unwilling to make changes that will draw younger people.

While this scenario sounds dismal, all is not lost. Help is available. In addition to church partnerships, pastors can as individuals affiliate with groups or fellowships that offer short-term missions assistance for programs, building projects, and community outreach. One such fellowship is the Cooperative Baptist Fellowship (CBF), which offers information regarding church partnerships, ministry grants, and discipleship training materials. Other denominations may have Christian groups that are willing to come and help churches to fulfill ministry goals within the church itself and the broader community.

In summary, How shall we get there? First and foremost, the female minister desiring to become a senior pastor should be sure that her calling is from God. She should strive to be educationally equipped and connected with male and female mentors, colleagues, religious social networks, and denominational bodies. She needs to be patient yet persistent, open and flexible, prayerful and faithful while maintaining her femininity and avoiding being overly negative with a lone ranger mentality. Women pastors seeking encouragement while serving with limited resources should consider examples of churches partnering with each other for ministry support. Consider affiliating with fellowships or national bodies that provide short-term missions support, and reach out to area clergy for ideas and communion.

Clergywomen must find ways to encourage, lift, and support one another with prayer, resources, helpful hints, and words of caution and affirmation. In the words of an old Negro spiritual, "Walk together children, don't you get weary; there's a great camp meeting in the Promised Land!"[22]

"Now faith is the substance of things hoped for, the evidence of things not seen. For by it the elders obtained a good report" (Hebrews 11:1-2, KJV).

Notes

1. Cynthia Bowers, "Breaking the Stained Glass Ceiling," *CBS Evening News Report,* Chicago, February 11, 2009,

http://www.cbsnews.com/8301-18563_162-3486335.html (accessed November 21, 2012).

2. The Fund for Theological Education, "The Basics: Theological Schools and Degrees," http://theoledu.bluestatedigi tal.com/preview/pages/96 (accessed November 21, 2012).

3. "The Basics."

4. "The Basics."

5. "The Basics."

6. "The Basics."

7. "The Basics."

8. "The Basics."

9. "The Basics."

10. "The Basics."

11. Christine A. Smith, "The Power of Perception and Denial," part 3, Ageism, interview with Rev. Julia Moses, http://shepastor.blogspot.com/2010/07/power-of-perception-and-denial-part-iii.html (accessed November 21, 2012).

12. Christine A. Smith, interview with Mamie Oliver, telephone interview, Cleveland, Ohio, May 2010.

13. Christine A. Smith, interview with Marilyn Parker-Jeffries, Cleveland, Ohio, February 2012.

14. Mary Ellen Konleczny and Mark Chaves, "Resources, Race, and Female-Headed Congregations in the United States," *Journal for the Scientific Study of Religion* 39, no. 3 (Spring 2000): 261.

15. John Dart, "Breaking Glass Ceilings at Large Churches," *Christian Century,* June 30, 2009, 15.

16. Susan Beaumont, "Inside the Large Congregation: Too Few Women," *Women in Leadership,* May 26, 2011, http://insidethe largecongregation.wordpress.com/tag/women-in-leadership/ (accessed November 21, 2012).

17. Christine A. Smith, interview with Debora Jackson, e-mail interview, March 2012.

18. Wilma R. Johnson, *Giving Away My Joy: The Psalmist Model of Spiritual Joy: A Commentary on Pastoral Leadership* (Lithonia, GA: Orman Press, 2005), 80–85.

19. Christine A. Smith, interview with Portia Wills Lee, telephone interview, August 2010.

20. Christine A. Smith, interview with Robin E. Hedgeman, Cleveland, Ohio June 2010.

21. Ebenezer Cobham Brewer, *Dictionary of Phrase and Fable*, "The Story of Stone Soup" (Philadelphia: Henry Altemus Company, 1898), www.Bartelby.com (accessed November 21, 2012).

22. Traditional, "A Great Camp-Meeting in the Promised Land."

SECTION TWO

Beyond the Ceiling

CHAPTER 5

What Will We Find There?

All these people earned a good reputation because of their faith, yet none of them received all that God had promised. For God had something better in mind for us, so that they would not reach perfection without us. (Hebrews 11:39-40, NLT)

In the words of the late Dr. Elton Trueblood, every generation has the bittersweet task of "planting shade trees under which we know full well we shall never sit." To plant them with joy or resentment is a choice. Pride, pain, regret, and bitterness at times prevent persons with a wealth of wisdom and experience from helping those who are coming after. I remember a stinging experience I had as a seminary student. I was given an assignment to contact a prominent female pastor to speak with her about her church's outreach ministry. To my surprise, she agreed to speak with me, but with great hostility she yelled over the phone,

> I started this church when nobody wanted to have anything to do with me! They didn't believe in women preachers. Why do they want to know how I do what I do? Where were all of you when I was working hard in the community and doing outreach to the poor?

Where were you when I started a food pantry and a clothes closet?

After going on and on for a few more minutes she abruptly hung up. Clearly the pains of rejection had not healed. Even the high level of success she had achieved did not assuage the wounds she endured as a woman rejected and denied, having to start a church because no church would give her a chance despite her qualifications.

If individuals are honest, it can be hurtful to realize and accept that some ceilings will not be broken during their lifetime. Women in ministry are still blazing trails, as it were. Women can, however, take the proverbial mallet in their hands, determine to join together, and beat upon the glass ceiling to make a million cracks. They must decide that the hardships they have endured will not embitter them but instead will embolden them to help bring about a change. Harlem Renaissance writer Zora Neale Hurston declared, "Mama exhorted her children at every opportunity to 'jump at de sun.' We might not land on the sun, but at least we would get off the ground."[1]

They must decide that the hardships they have endured will not embitter them but instead will embolden them to help bring about a change.

At a seminar for female clergy titled "Breaking the Stained Glass Ceiling," one of the presenters reiterated a notion discussed earlier: Women don't ask. The basic point of her message was that women, because of their proclivity for nurturing, supporting, and making do, tend to accept less and are expected to expect less in terms of salary, benefits, church growth (numerically), and opportunities.

The presenter made a distinction between sinful ambition and holy ambition. Sinful ambition was described as selfish in nature: the attitude that "it's all about me," my goals, my desires, my benefits. Holy ambition was described as a desire to grow, thrive, and obtain not only for self but also for the furthering of God's kingdom. In other words, holy ambition has a view toward increased resources for increased opportunities to minister. This does not suggest that it is sinful to desire opportunities commensurate with education and experience. It is not sinful to desire decent pay, benefits, and a vacation. Nor is it sinful to desire to serve in a larger venue if you feel led or called to do so.

To expand upon these issues, consider the following quote:

> For women who aspire to leadership positions in church organizations, the career path can be a lonely one, with few role models and mentors. Overall, women lead about 8 percent of congregations, and only about 5 percent of American churchgoers attend a congregation led by a woman, according to the National Congregations Study. The study also found that women who work as pastors are less likely to report satisfaction with their jobs than their male colleagues. The challenge is how to do the job in new ways. . . . Women have responded to this need in different ways, including conferences, formal church programs and online chat rooms and blogs. In these formal and informal spaces, women clergy are coming together to connect with and support one another.[2]

The author, Natalie Gott, goes on to describe four examples of clergywomen networking with each other. One example is the Lead Women Pastors Project, designed to identify female clergy who desire and have the potential to lead large (1,000+) congregations.

Case Study: Lead Women Pastors Project

The Lead Women Pastors Project offers powerful examples of how women pastors of larger congregations can serve as mentors for others. One such pastor, Rev. Karen Oliveto, has served in a variety of ministries including urban, rural, and campus ministries. At Gott's writing, Oliveto was serving in San Francisco as co-pastor of Glide Memorial Church's eleven-thousand-member congregation. Women in Rev. Oliveto's position have found it difficult to find other female mentors and colleagues as they advance in the ministry.

According to Gott, Rev. Oliveto's role in the project will be to help provide mentorship for other women. The project pairs twenty-five women who, like Oliveto, serve churches with one thousand or more members, with twenty-five women who have been identified by United Methodist bishops as having the potential to one day lead a church of that size.

The coaches meet with their partners at least once a month for two years. The coaches also participate in groups and individual training sessions designed to help the pastors in the program determine if their gifts are a match for leading a large church. "What I hope to offer is to help another clergy woman come into a fuller sense of her own power and authority," said Oliveto.[3]

Another phase of the Lead Women Pastors Project called for female and male senior pastors of large United Methodist congregations to be surveyed on a variety of issues, targeting leadership styles. They discovered that women who lead large churches are still pioneers. Gott's article revealed that nine out of ten women were the first females to lead their large congregations. Furthermore, the study showed that 77 percent of women pastors leading large churches developed their leadership styles from their mentors and role models. The Lead Women Pastors Project embraces the mentorship model and seeks to create greater opportunities for women to pastor larger congregations.[4]

What an opportunity for women in ministry! It would be wonderful if the idea of mentoring clergywomen to become senior
pastors of larger congregations would blossom and spread
beyond churches that are hierarchical in nature, such as
Methodist or Episcopal, to churches that are congregational in
nature, such as Baptist.

A Cloud of Witnesses

Considering further what we will find there, it is important to hear
the testimonies of women who are there. Surveyed clergywomen
shared the following in response to the question, "What is the
greatest challenge you face being a female senior pastor?"

> My challenges are not just because I am a female pastor.
> The challenges that I face are financial, and that could be
> [true of] male or female [pastors]. Strictly speaking there
> are no challenges that I face other than being a female and
> a wife. I have double duty. I can't just go home after
> preaching on Sunday or teaching Bible study. I have a
> household to keep up, chores to do, and a daytime job.
> Also, when invited out to preach, women are not paid as
> much as the brothers even when we have more education
> and are well able to bring a powerful word. — *Virginia*

> When I started in ministry, it was the absolute sense of iso-
> lation and lack of preparation and resources. Now, I
> think most of my struggles are similar to [those of] my
> male colleagues: unrealistic/unfair expectations from the
> church, dysfunctional people, church conflict, pressures
> of leading the church during an era of great change. I still
> find individuals who have an issue with my gender, and

relationships with more traditional women in my church seem most difficult. I also feel a lot of sadness about the lack of options for me after this pastorate. I love being a pastor but doubt that an appropriate position will be there for me. —*Ohio*

For me, it is establishing boundaries that would help prevent overextending myself. As females, we are so gifted with multitasking that it is a blessing and yet it is a curse, because we are able to do it so effectively and well that we have a tendency to take on much more than is healthy for us. We have the responsibility of taking care of home, church, children, and so we, like the "Energizer bunny," keep going and going and going until the battery runs dry. As a single mother, I never wanted my daughter to feel that I had put the church before her. Her biological father is deceased; therefore, she had only one parent. Being the mother of a one-parent child, I probably over extended myself because I never wanted her to feel neglected. I wanted her to have a parent there to share with her in day-to-day experiences during the years of her life. —*Georgia*

Getting opportunities. One of the major reasons I was called to my current church is that I have been ministering in the area for over twenty years—mostly in chaplaincy. I have gotten to know churches as part of serving as the denominational facilitator and there were churches who would never have considered a woman but who considered me as a known quantity. I think I would have a lot of trouble finding a church if I were to leave this area. Sometimes, although I do find the men in most pastorates in the area are supportive of me, there is not the fellowship that they have among themselves, and there are not enough women to have a comparable group for me. —*Pennsylvania*

Biblical Encouragement

Many of the challenges expressed so far are related to practical matters: having to juggle numerous responsibilities and minimal resources, setting boundaries, and feeling overwhelmed. Although they are not specifically stated, several underlying challenges appear to be psychological in nature. Overcoming feelings of guilt due to decreased time spent with family, frustration over pay inequities, and isolation all can take a toll on a person's heart and mind. For those feeling buried by these realities, I offer words of encouragement and advice from Scripture:

> Let us draw near to God with a sincere heart in full assurance of faith, having our hearts sprinkled to cleanse us from a guilty conscience and having our bodies washed with pure water. Let us hold unswervingly to the hope we profess, for he who promised is faithful. And let us consider how we may spur one another on toward love and good deeds. (Hebrews 10:22-24, NIV)

In this passage of Scripture, the writer encourages us with three phrases.

"Let Us Draw Near to God"
Even as preachers of the gospel, we can be drawn away from the true source of our strength, joy, peace, and fulfillment in life. Hectic schedules filled with family obligations, counseling sessions, preaching engagements, board and community meetings, individual projects, and myriad other things can drain us of vitality. When

we are tired, our guard is down. Overburdened hearts and minds leave little room for the refreshing Word that comes only from spending time with the Lord. So often we stand and deliver words of faith, hope, and encouragement when our own reservoir is depleted. Frustration, doubt, fear, and even guilt can begin to loom over us.

Marching orders. Draw near to God! Move forward, not backward. Move toward the Lord. Seek God's face. Study God's Word, not just for sermon preparation but to discern God's leading in every situation and circumstance in your life. "Draw nigh to God, and he will draw nigh to you" (James 4:8, KJV).

"Let Us Hold Unswervingly to the Hope We Profess"
Are you swerving due to discouragement? Do you allow doubt to cloud your vision, dowse your enthusiasm, strangle your joy? If we do not nurture and build our relationship with the Lord Jesus Christ, with continual prayer, personal study, fellowship with other women and men of God, and healthy activities, our faith will begin to falter and our grip on "the hope we profess" can become loose. Our positions as preachers, teachers, and leaders can set us up for swerving. We are so busy pouring into the lives of others that we can swerve off the path of faith.

Ministry has had many casualties—women and men who started out with energy, vision, promise, and purpose but somehow swerved and fell backwards. Seasons of drought—plowing, planting, praying, and seeing few results; or super success—times of bountiful blessings and abundance with the temptations of pride and self-indulgence—somehow loosened the grip of their hold to God's unchanging hands, and they fell backwards.

Marching orders. Hold fast to the profession of your faith, remembering that the God "who promised" is faithful. God is faithful. God will not forget your labor of love. God is faithful— all God's promises are true. God is faithful. Earthly abundance cannot compare with the blessings God has for those who endure until the end. Don't you want to stand with the great cloud of witnesses and proclaim, "I have fought a good fight, I have finished my course, I have kept the faith" (2 Timothy 4:7, KJV)? You have come this far; don't give up now!

"Let Us Consider How We May Spur One Another On"
We need each other. We need support, encouragement, challenge, and at times confrontation to help us to be all that we are called to be. The dynamics of community, a healthy, God-led community, can "spur us on" to "love and good deeds." Isolation contributes to unhealthy patterns of thinking. We become inwardly focused and susceptible to depression, resentment, and lack of forgiveness. Too much time alone can cause you to dwell too deeply upon the past, hurts, mistakes, or regrets. In loving community, we have the opportunity to process our feelings, share our thoughts, and receive feedback and guidance that may help us make better choices and decisions.

Who is in this community? Whoever you can trust to see you not only as clergy but also as a human being. Prayerfully develop a community made up of individuals who can hear your joys and not be jealous, listen to your struggles and not be offended, and empathize with your pain and not lose respect for your position. This kind of community is not easily developed. It takes prayer, time, discernment, and perseverance. It may take a while, but don't give up. God has others who are looking for the same kind of support and encouragement. Through perseverance and faith, find each other.

Marching orders. Encourage one another to love and do what is right in God's eyes. In community we can help each other to move forward, keep the faith, persevere, remain hopeful, let go of the past, and forgive. "Onward Christian soldiers, marching as to war, with the cross of Jesus going on before."[5]

Additional specific recommendations regarding how we as female pastors can safeguard our hearts against psychological, spiritual, and emotional attacks are given in chapter 6, "Who Shall We Become There?"

Good News about Ministry

While the challenges appear daunting, they are not the only defining characteristic of respondent expressions. The pastorate also provided some pleasant surprises for those surveyed. After hearing many of the challenges, some women developed an assumption that support would be minimal, the path would be predominantly doom and gloom, and the struggle would be unbearable. Others have experienced the opposite. In response to the question, "What has been the most eye-opening experience for you as a female senior pastor?" survey respondents wrote:

> Finding encouragement and support from male senior pastors. The congregation realizing that even though you are paid for twenty hours, you are actually working forty to sixty hours. —*New Hampshire*

> Sometimes people are supporting me in quiet ways. They may not overtly express their feelings, but when difficulties or confrontations arise, they will make their love, confidence, and support of me as a pastor known. Sometimes they will send me a card. Sometimes when I least expect it, they will stand up for a project or program that has been questioned. —*Ohio*

> The Lord gives me a sermon to preach every Sunday!
> —*Ohio*

Even though I serve a small congregation, we are able to accomplish many things through local mission outreach. —*Massachusetts*

Leaving the church I served. I did not realize how stressed and angry I had become. I also did not realize how internally focused I was. I now realize I had allowed the church to limit my vision for ministry. —*Indiana*

After a Christmas Eve service in which I had preached, I was approached by a congregant who thanked me for bringing a "woman's perspective" to the story of the nativity. It was eye-opening in that I had not made any overt effort to preach as a woman but simply preached from the text as usual for me, which, it turned out, brought a point of view otherwise absent from this individual's experience. There also have been other moments when I have suspected I am welcomed in because of my gender. There may be a perception that I possess a certain level of sensitivity because I am a woman. —*Connecticut*

Life would never be the same. I had such a carefree life as a flight attendant. It is no longer the same because of the light of Christ that we carry. Every place you go, people see that light, and you are never off duty. You become the counselor, the advisor, a little of everything to everybody whether they are members of your congregation or not, whether they know that you pastor or not. Sometimes, I and my daughter are out and someone will begin to talk to me about the woes of life. I was not aware that it would be this way. When I became a pastor, it brought about a greater awareness of the responsibility of being a pastor. —*Georgia*

When people get past the whole "woman pastor thing," they tend to be very receptive. I found certainly when I was doing chaplaincy that more people felt free to really express their hurt and pain with me than with their male pastor. As a senior pastor, it is having to remind the young boys that they can be pastors too! —*Pennsylvania*

Amid the pain and struggle, God still provides springs in the desert. Isaiah 35:1 (KJV) declares, "The wilderness and the dry land shall be glad for them; and the desert shall rejoice, and blossom as the rose." At times, ministry may feel like a desert. Yet even the parched, cracked, prickly experiences of a female pastor's struggle cannot thwart God's blessings, God's roses, God's designated seasons of refreshing and renewal for her. As the roots of the cactus search for the reservoirs of water that lie deep beneath the desert floor, so women in ministry must allow their roots to go deeper through prayer, study, fellowship, and perseverance.

God also provides us with another metaphor for resiliency during seasons of struggle. Psalm 1:3 (KJV) declares, "And he shall be like a tree planted by the rivers of water, that bringeth forth his fruit in his season; his leaf also shall not wither; and whatsoever he doeth shall prosper." When I was growing up in Ohio, I remember frigid temperatures, heavy snowfalls, snow days (which we as children loved!), and cups of hot cocoa. But last winter was exceptionally mild: thirties through the high forties were the average temperatures. Some people expressed concern that if the flowers bloomed too early and winter came back, the cold temperatures would freeze and kill them. One morning I took a brief walk through my family's garden. Sure enough, tulip leaves, buttercup stems, and the rose bush were all beginning to sprout. As I stared at the beautiful green shoots, the tiny leaves pushing through the cold dirt, I began to contemplate God's message as revealed through nature.

God has given us metaphors for resiliency. Planted deep into the soil, covered with dirt and fertilizer, the flowers remain in the ground during the cold winter. In God's own time, however, the sun rises, the hard ground softens, and the flowers push through all the mess to break forth into glorious blossoms. Plants and flowers must be resilient. Their growth pushes them up and out, beyond the dirt that is piled upon them. They ignore the threat of a return to cold weather. They trust the sun.

Many people, especially clergywomen, have experienced being piled upon. Some feel buried beneath so much stuff that they are unable to push through. Is that you? Are you afraid to press upward for fear of being annihilated by the cold, whatever your cold may be? I encourage you to consider the flowers and trust the Son. As the plants and flowers feel the sun and push through the dirt, you and I can trust the Son and push through, push past, and stand on top of whatever has sought to weigh us down.

Gardeners will sometimes place a tarp over their tender shoots so that frost won't kill them. God too sees our eagerness to push out from under the heavy weight that is stifling us. If it is too soon for us to come out, God's Holy Spirit will cover us. Sometimes we become angry and anxious because we want out. But the Lord's tarp is covering us until our due season. Sometimes we think it is time, but our times are in God's hands (Psalm 31:15). Keep pushing upward. Push past dirt, pain, dysfunction, anxiety, depression, regret, turmoil, whatever is pressing you down. Be resilient like the flowers. In God's time your blossoms will break forth. Your leaf will not wither, and you will prosper. It must be understood that perception is half the battle. Stay the course. God is faithful.

As the roots of the cactus search for the reservoirs of water that lie deep beneath the desert floor, so women in ministry must allow their roots to go deeper through prayer, study, fellowship, and perseverance.

As women in ministry grapple with the various issues regarding the pastorate, I thought it would be helpful to those coming along to hear insights that those currently serving wished others had shared with them. Survey participants were asked to complete the following statement, "Before becoming a pastor, I wish I was told . . ." They responded in a variety of ways.

Find female friends. Don't forget about family, and make time for myself. —*Ohio*

How to negotiate compensation and salary packages. —*New Hampshire*

Don't think you are going to change the congregation in the first couple years. It won't happen! It may never happen. That while numbers are important to "the system," it's really all about changing hearts and deepening relationships with God—both theirs AND YOURS! —*New Jersey*

That pastoring is a journey of learning to trust God in every situation, to love the people no matter what, to listen for the Spirit's voice, to believe God's promises, and to cling to Christ the Vine who produces spiritual fruit through the branches. —*New York*

Not to take criticism as an assault on who I am as a person or even as a pastor. To see beyond the comment and look for the issue the person is dealing with.
—*Massachusetts*

What will be found on the other side of the stained glass ceiling? You will find encouragement and challenge in, an increasing number of mentors and sisters who understand the struggle and who are working to identify strategies and methods to expand the opportunities available for women in ministry and hope for a brighter future. You will also face the realities of pioneers—naysayers, rough ministerial terrain, periods of loneliness and trial, and forks in the road.

With faith and determination, we must learn to embrace the words found in Hebrews 12:2-3 (KJV): "looking unto Jesus the author and the finisher of our faith, who for the joy that was set before him, endured the cross, despising the shame. . . . Consider him who endured such contradictions of sinners against himself, lest you become weary and faint in your mind."

So often, the challenges of the ministry can create feelings of defeat within us. I have found, however, that making a decision to be thankful even in the midst of dark hours can raise our hearts to levels of victory and trump defeat. Being thankful is a choice. It is not always an easy choice. Human frailty draws our focus toward what is not right rather than right, what is not fair rather than fair, what is hurtful and bad rather than what is healing and beautiful. A friend of mine once described it this way: "Our perception of life can be like two buckets of water—one filled and one with barely a drop. As blessings are thrown into our full bucket, they just make ripples. But when proverbial rocks are thrown into the almost empty bucket, they make a very loud noise."

So many blessings plop into our full bucket that we barely notice them. When bad things happen, they make a loud, clanging noise, and we are drawn to focus upon them. We can, however, choose to be thankful. We must learn to praise God in advance. When we choose thanks and praise over frustration, over anger, over focusing upon all that is wrong, we trump Satan's attempts to defeat us. Our praise and thanks confuse the enemy. When we choose thanks and praise over focusing upon the things that are wrong in our lives, we position ourselves for triumph over our circumstances. Let us "lay aside" and "throw off" everything that hinders our praise and fix our eyes upon Jesus, remembering the great cloud of witnesses not only in the Bible but also in our own lives, and thank God for all that God has already done. In the face of discouragement, closed doors, and glass ceilings, don't faint. Remember Jesus. Through him, all things are possible!

Notes

1. A. P. Porter, *Jump at de Sun: The Story of Zora Neale Hurston,* (Minneapolis, MN: Lerner Publishing Group, Inc.) 1992, 16.

2. Natalie Gott, "Clergy Women Make Connections," *Faith and Leadership* [an online journal of Duke Divinity School], February 16, 2010, http://www.faithandleadership.com/features/aticles/clergy-women-make-connections (accessed November 23, 2012).

3. Gott, "Clergy Women Make Connections."

4. Gott, "Clergy Women Make Connections."

5. Sabine Baring-Gould, "Onward Christian Soldiers" (1865).

CHAPTER 6

Who Shall We Become There?

To every thing there is a season, and a time to every purpose under the heaven. (Ecclesiastes 3:1, KJV)

Whether a pastor is male or female, maintaining balance between family life and ministry is essential. Female pastors in particular must be intentional about finding and keeping a healthy balance. Male clergy often have elements in place that many clergywomen are not privileged to receive. There is a social psychological dynamic at play that fosters support and even sympathy for male pastors that frequently does not exist for females.

Mothers of the church tend to adopt the male pastors as sons and therefore seek to assist them, their wives, and their children in a number of ways. Frequently laity, particularly women, will dote over the male pastor and seek to enter the inner circle of the first lady. Offers to babysit the children, prepare meals, take clothing to the dry cleaners, bake delicacies, drive the pastor to and from meetings, or type additional work are not uncommon. Female pastors are often viewed differently.

Women tend to be adept at multitasking. However, this giftedness can do a disservice to us through workaholism and the perception by other females that we can "handle it." The lack of support may not be intentional, which might be more dangerous. There may be no thought given to our needs. There should be an intentional awareness of our pastoral, professional, and personal necessities. Since this sensitivity may not come naturally, female pastors must take the somewhat uncomfortable initiative and encourage, teach, and cultivate an atmosphere of support.

We must wisely cultivate support and negotiate policies and procedures that promote our physical, mental, and emotional health. We must establish boundaries such as identifying specific times for pastoral visits and phone calls (understanding there must be flexibility for emergencies—but every day should not have an emergency) or scheduling vacation weeks and taking them. If possible, we should nurture the development of a pastor's aide ministry that assists with special tasks such as offering to have the pastor's robes dry cleaned, providing babysitting once or twice a month so the pastor and her spouse can go out to dinner, and highlighting pastor appreciation week, during which the congregation is encouraged to share cards, tokens of appreciation, and kind words. While these suggestions may appear self-serving, they go a long way to assist the congregation in seeing the pastor as a human being, called by God to serve as shepherd but still needing support and appreciation. The healthier the pastor, the greater service she can provide in ministering to the flock.

Prior to accepting a congregational call, a female pastor should examine the church's administrative structure and discuss her administrative style and expectations as well as those of the church. Avoid being so eager to pastor that you jump into a fire pit! If you accept a fiery situation, be very sure that the Lord has called you there. If so, God will give you the wisdom, endurance, and faith to overcome each circumstance. In any case, expectations on both ends should be clear. If possible, work through discrepancies and put decisions in writing before entering into any contractual agreements. Watch for contracts that demand a heavy workload for the pastor but allow little voice, authority, or input from the pastor. Many pastors, men and women, have experienced broken and bruised spirits because they have worked themselves tirelessly and found themselves with little or no authority to change unhealthy structures in the church.

One of my male clergy mentors once shared with me in a private conversation his experience with such an unhealthy structure:

> I was invited to interview as a candidate for a prominent church in another city. As I sat in the interview and read over the administrative structure of the church, I noticed that the office of the pastor was number 16 on the hierarchical list! I said to myself, "Why in the world would I leave the church where I know that I am the pastor and am respected as such to go to a place where the office of the pastor is number 16?"

What can be gleaned from this insight is the importance of understanding administrative structures and recognizing potential hazards in terms of challenges to pastoral leadership and authority. If a female pastor has not had the privilege of working alongside a strong pastor or at least had the opportunity to observe strong pastoral leaders, she may be oblivious to some of the ins and outs of working with congregations in general and lay leaders in particular. Learning the history, underpinnings, power players, tendencies, and trends of a congregation are all critical considerations for a pastor prior to accepting a call to a church.

A minister can research a congregation's history, members' demographics, characteristics, and relationship with previous pastors in several ways.

■ *Have a conversation with the area or executive minister.* Ask questions such as the length or tenure of prior pastors in that church and reasons for separation (e.g., retirement, death, termination, resignation).

■ *Request to see the church bulletin and church history.* Many churches have their history posted on their websites. Reading about a church's history can provide valuable information such as the role(s) that individuals and families played in developing and sustaining the congregation, their mission and vision, their priorities in terms of ministry, edifice, and community involvement. Most churches also have a bulletin. This will provide information about their current worship structure, music style, and technology.

■ *Ask to see a copy of the church constitution.* This will provide information concerning the church polity, governance, administrative structure, and pastoral and staff positions.

■ *Ask to see a copy of the church budget.* This will also provide a sense of the congregation's priorities, areas for growth, and overall stewardship.

■ *If it is a local congregation, talk with family and friends about the nature of the congregation.* What is the reputation of the church and its members?

These recommendations are meant to give examples of how to gain some insight about a congregation if one is being considered to serve as pastor. These factors are also important for building a healthy relationship with a congregation, should the call to serve be accepted. In the words of Proverbs, "Wisdom is the principal thing; therefore get wisdom: and with all thy getting get understanding" (Proverbs 4:7, KJV).

In smaller congregations, there is a tendency on the part of the female pastor to seek to be all things to all people. If she is married, she strives to be an attentive wife and homemaker (as should be the case). If she is wife and mother, she strives to be a mother who spends quantity and quality time with her children, juggling church meetings and school plays, community events with concerts or athletic games, and sermons with book reports. If she has adult children, she may find herself trying to support them if they are out of work, counseling them if they are having relationship problems, or making time to babysit grandchildren. If her parents are still living, frequently she will do her utmost to ensure their well-being. That may mean scheduling doctor appointments and maybe even taking them to the doctor and being sure they have groceries, clean clothes, cooked meals, and a ride to church. If they are ill, it may mean frequent visits to the hospital or nursing home, coordinating services with doctors and social workers, and being sure they are receiving the proper care. All of this is done in addition to caring for her flock.

If she is not careful, the female pastor can be drawn into becoming the chief bottle washer, floor sweeper, bulletin and bulletin board maker, food pantry operator, transportation ministry leader, special event coordinator, twenty-four-hour on-call chaplain, and official "fire putter outer."

A survey respondent from Ohio commented:

> One of the struggles that I had in pursuing ministry was my age, fifty. Prior to retiring, I was bi-vocational, balancing work and ministry. I had an aging mother, who was a widow with Alzheimer's. She lived to see me be licensed and preach my initial sermon, but not my ordination. I am learning how important it is to carve out time for myself and be intentional. I'm still not doing it as well as I should. There are times when I still don't have a day off even though I've retired from my secular job. Part of my issue is that I'm a perfectionist and I just want things right. Since my office is at home, I have to be intentional about not going into my office. My husband plays a big part in saying, "Turn off that computer and SIT DOWN!"

Some female pastors have said, "I do everything because there is nobody else to help." Recently, at a conference for women in ministry, pastors shared their frustration over having so few resources that they felt the need to cover most bases themselves. One pastor said that she gets up extra early to pick up several members of her congregation so that they have a ride to church. Another pastor said that she is suffering from burnout while doing the work of a pastor, secretary, food pantry coordinator, and clothes distributor. Another spoke of the difficulty of having a dilapidated building and not enough monies for repairs.

At the same meeting, a panel discussed how women could creatively handle the stress of their situations. As the floor became open for questions and answers, a few pastors began to ask about the availability of grant monies for special programming, assistance for practical matters such as building repairs, vans for transportation ministries, and assistance with secretarial support. Several women vehemently opposed the idea that more financial assistance was needed. They also began to defend their unhealthy practices of doing all that they were doing, justifying their choices with, "The Lord was giving me the strength to do it, and the people were being helped!"

It was almost as though these women felt the need to bear the unreasonable and devastatingly heavy load to prove their faithfulness. If other avenues for assistance and support have been thoroughly explored and no help is available, extreme dedication is faithfulness. If a woman has resigned herself to handling most everything on her own without truly investigating other avenues of support, it is suicide.

Female pastors must be careful not to adopt the savior mentality. Jesus Christ is the Savior. Pastors need to point others to Jesus. If a pastor is stretched to the limit, fatigued, and in denial about being depressed, it will be nearly impossible to preach, teach, and minister as one has been called to do. Therefore, women pastors must learn the necessary art of delegation. We must pray and ask the Lord to help us to discern the gifts and talents within our churches and broader community. It may appear easier to do the work ourselves rather than taking the time to identify, nurture, build, and train others, but in the long run, doing so will pay off. Surely God has placed others in the congregation or surrounding areas who can perform at least two or three of the tasks that the pastor has unwisely taken on.

There must be resistance to the temptation to operate in a codependent fashion. In other words, do not allow the need to feel wanted to aid and abet an atmosphere of helplessness in the congregation. But rather, teach, "I can do all things through Christ who strengthens me" (Philippians 4:13, NRSV).

Pastor Jacquelyn Ragin Olds shared these words of wisdom in response to the question, "What kind of support base have you developed to maintain mental, spiritual, and physical health?"

> I can't overemphasize the need for advisors/mentors who will provide some support and guidance. Every pastor needs a spiritual guide. I don't care who you are or how much God uses you. Also, I have a network of like-minded Christian women—some ministers, some not. I work out three or four times a week, even it if is just taking a walk for physical health. I watch what I eat even if I have to put the fruits and vegetables in a blender and drink them on the way to work! I think most important for me is the renewing of my mind. The renewing of my mind gets lost in the busyness. It is the first thing that gets sacrificed if I am not careful. I have to read and meditate upon God's Word every day to stay spiritually healthy. If I am overly busy it is the first thing that gets compromised.
>
> I listen to other pastors and preachers. I don't just want to hear myself every day. Seminary is a good experience. I

know some people are scared of seminary, but I feel that it is a must. You can find advisors, mentors, like-minded Christian women, and resources to renew your mind. It is a good place. Keep the vision in front of you so you will stay excited and be less likely to wander. Have some prayer partners who understand what you are trying to do. That is real important. Wait on the Lord because God's timing is important. God's timing may not be your timing. Keep it simple initially.

Don't take on too much, or too many duties or projects. Just stick to one or two. Don't be envious of other ministries because that is like having weak ankles. You've got this wonderful, able body. You can do all things through Christ who strengthens you, but if your ankles are weak, you will stumble at an inopportune time. God needs you to be yourself. One of the first things God said to me after I became a pastor was, "You be you—I need you to be you."[1] —*Ohio*

Issues of Marriage for Female Pastors

During a marriage counseling session between a clergywoman and her fiancé, a wise pastor said, "The Lord might call your wife to pastor one day. Can you handle that?" To which her beloved quickly responded, "YES!" This man was familiar with female pastors. His grandmother was a Methodist pastor, and his great-aunt was a bishop in a nondenominational church. The pastor raised important questions that helped to lay the groundwork for a successful partnership in the ministry. The female pastor was grateful that her husband had never done anything to hinder the work of ministry the Lord entrusted to her. Although she had to leave a large, Spirit-filled, energetic ministry (one in which her husband had been a member for more than thirty years) to pastor in a very different setting, he never complained. He never emanated resentment or anger and continues to do all that he can to support her. Not all female ministers are as fortunate.

While many women have stood by the side of their husbands who felt called to pastor, even if it meant going to a street corner and setting up chairs, some women have a different experience. There is much heartache experienced by many female clergy as they bemoan the lack of support from their spouses. Some have said that when they were invited to candidate for a church, they were told by their husband, "If that church calls you, you are going by yourself! This is *my* church—I'm not going anywhere!" At that point, the woman is confronted with a difficult decision: pursue her calling and risk losing her marriage or let the call go and seethe with resentment. She can pray and trust the Lord to change her husband's heart, but that can take years. Either way, it is an unwelcome battle.

Other women have contended with the jealousy and insecurities of their spouses. As one clergywoman said, "It was eye-opening to experience my husband's jealousy about me pastoring."

If a female pastor and her spouse came from a church where her husband held a prominent position, such as a deacon or trustee, it may be even more difficult for him to leave and go with her to a new ministry. The husband of a female pastor must be secure in himself. Insensitive comments such as, "Your wife must wear the pants in your family. Why are you following her? Isn't she supposed to follow you?" and "He must be henpecked" cannot deter his support for his wife and the work to which she has been called. When and wherever possible, the spouse should be encouraged to use his gifts and talents in the ministry. In addition to supporting the pastor, he can derive a sense of purpose and satisfaction from fulfilling his God-given calling and contributing to the work of the church.

There are male spouses who provide wonderful support to their wives who pastor. One female pastor's husband said,

> I see my role as her supporter. It is my responsibility to be sure that she has everything she needs to do the work that the Lord has called her to do. I don't want to do anything to stand in her way. It would be nice to meet other men whose wives are pastors. Sometimes I'm not sure how to respond or what to do because there are so few of us.

Some pastors' husbands in the Cleveland, Ohio, region are beginning to discuss forming their own support group to address their unique needs. It can be awkward for male spouses. For example, at ministerial functions when the master of ceremonies announces, "Would all of the ministers' wives please stand?" or, "Would all the ministers' wives meet afterward to discuss the upcoming Christmas dinner?" what are the men to do? Most often they bow their heads and chuckle in embarrassment. For this reason, many female pastors find themselves attending functions alone. There is a need to remind ministerial groups that there are increasing numbers of female pastors with husbands. Therefore, events should address and include male and female spouses.

Clergy Couples

For female pastors who are married to male pastors serving in a different congregation, the balancing act can be a challenge in many areas. Depending upon the times of their services, the two pastors may find themselves at different churches preaching, teaching, and performing other duties simultaneously. Both may be drained when they come home, both may have war stories to share as well as praise reports, and neither may feel like cooking dinner, washing clothes, or walking the dog.

One might say, "Well, what is the difference between two pastors and two people going to work every day?" Pastoring is more than a job. It is a life work. It involves dealing with the heart, mind, and soul of individuals, families, and even communities. The pay may be low or unstable. If their congregations belong to different conventions or denominational affiliates, their board meetings or annual congresses may vary, requiring separate vacations or trips if schedules cannot be reconciled.

One female pastor whose husband pastored a different church commented, "My service is held earlier than his, so when I get through preaching, I take off my robe, head over to his church, sit in the front pew, and put on my 'first lady' hat!" Another female pastor said that she and her husband, who pastors at a different church in the same city, have agreed that neither of them would accept a call to another congregation unless it was in the same city or unless the new church was willing to call them as co-pastors. Trying to maintain a marriage while living in two separate cities and pastoring two separate congregations can be dangerous.

On the positive side, having someone who can intimately understand and relate to the struggles of pastoring can be a blessing. Another female pastor said, "My husband and I have so much to talk about. We share stories about how we are dealing with various issues that arise in our congregations, ministry program ideas, and administrative issues. It is wonderful having someone at home who can totally relate to what I'm going through."

In "Effective Clergy Couples," Kathleen Bostrom shared this bit of advice:

> Serving as a clergy couple has its difficulties. Greg and I find that our conversations with each other are often

dominated by church business. One night while lying in bed, we found ourselves talking about the day at church: the person we saw in the hospital, the elder who had personal problems, the family that hadn't been in church for a while. Suddenly we realized what we were doing. We had invited the congregation into our bedroom! So one by one, we told them to leave. "Get out of here, Mary! Leave us alone, Joe!" We visualized them climbing off the bed and skulking out the door, slamming it behind them. Now we are more careful about protecting our private life.[2]

Bishop Elizabeth Eaton has spoken about the challenges of clergy couples as they balance the needs of their families and those of their congregations. She further explains that their lives may also be complicated by trying to find parishes in the same area or in geographical proximity. A plus for clergy couples is having a partner who knows and understands the demands of the pastorate. Bishop Eaton offered these words of wisdom and encouragement for clergy couples:

> We tell our clergy couples, and all clergy for that matter, to be very intentional about setting boundaries—when they are having time with their families and when they are having time with their congregations. Congregations that are served by a member of a clergy couple must also understand that the spouse of their pastor can't always be at the church. One of the keys is remembering the vows you made both to each other and to God.[3]

Balancing the weight of the pastorate between two ministers serving different congregations requires prayer, humility, compromise, organization, and flexibility.

Single Female Pastors

Many female pastors are single. Some are single by choice and some by circumstance such as widowhood or divorce. Some still hope to get married. According to survey respondents, the positive aspects of pastoring while single are many. They include freedom to move about geographically, no spouse or children to be concerned about protecting from the struggles of ministry, and no need to coordinate schedules with a family. These pastors are free to go about the work of the ministry without being concerned with how the demands will affect a household.

Challenges, however, do exist for the single female pastor. Many single female pastors experience difficulty finding someone to date. In the survey, approximately 72 percent agreed with the statement "It is difficult to find someone to date." Only 22.7 percent strongly disagreed. Many single female pastors struggle with feelings of loneliness and isolation. This is not to suggest that all single female pastors are lonely, but many have expressed this sentiment.

> Solo pastoring can be very lonely. I was married before I became a pastor. When I was married, we had a built-in relationship that allowed room for sharing frustrations, chuckles, progress, and highs and lows. Since being single, it has been a struggle to find the level of relational intimacy (relational, not sexual) and confidentiality with anyone. —*New Jersey*

> Because of my position as a senior pastor, men appear to be intimidated and reluctant to approach me for a date. —*California*

> I certainly don't want to date anyone in my congregation. If things went wrong that would be extremely awkward. —*Ohio*

> I sometimes struggle to figure out what is and is not appropriate in terms of finding a date. Of course I pray for the Lord's guidance, but still it can be difficult. I am leery of online dating services. —*Illinois*

If we are honest, dating can be a dilemma particularly for young, unmarried women who serve as pastors. Single clergywomen may be particularly sensitive to passages of Scripture such as 1 Thessalonians 4:3 (ESV), "For this is the will of God, your sanctification: that you abstain from sexual immorality," and 1 Thessalonians 5:22 (KJV), "Abstain from all appearance of evil." Single female pastors may fear appearing evil or without self-control if they are dating. They may struggle with managing their emotions regarding physical attraction toward their date. Single clergywomen may also experience having to calm the nervousness of a date who is trying to navigate intimacy with a preacher.

Pastor Wren Miller, a single female pastor of a megachurch in Huntsville, Alabama, shared some of her frustrations concerning dating as a clergywoman. She explains that during an evening out with her "cute" date, they began flirting with one another, admiring one another and were just about to kiss when her date stopped cold. With trepidation and alarm he pulled back and declared, "What if people see us?" Pastor Miller believed that her date's unease was not due to concerns about intimacy with a woman but rather intimacy with a woman pastor! She further explains her feelings of dismay . . .

> By night, I look like an average 27-year-old woman with my fitted jeans, hobo handbag, and sweeping blonde hair; but by day, I am a full-time pastor of a 3,000-member congregation. This means that nearly every Sunday, . . . you'll find me going up to the pulpit in a collar and cassock, my black ankle-length robe. With that not-so-sexy image

undoubtedly in mind, my date backed off. We never did kiss that night. And soon after, he stopped calling."[4]

Single clergywomen who want to date or court will have to learn the delicate balance of walking in their beauty, attractiveness, and femininity while maintaining respect as a pastor. They will also have to decide whether or not it is expedient to become involved with a member of their congregation. A pastor, male or female, should be very careful about dating a parishioner. If things do not work out, it can be devastating for the member, the pastor, and the congregation. Personal information could be spread and ruin a pastor's name, or the member may try to use sensitive information to control the pastor. Conversely, the member may become confused or distraught and leave the church. Much prayer and consideration must be given before such a relationship is initiated.

Not all single female clergy are interested in dating. Some just would enjoy companionship. While married clergy have someone to come home to and talk, share, pray, and laugh with, many single clergy find themselves coming home to an empty house with no one with whom to reflect, share, or vent. Many single female pastors have found wonderful ways to fill any void created by loneliness. Dinner with adopted families, recreational activities such as sports and sororities, hobbies, and special interests all help to keep feelings of isolation at bay. Whether a pastor is married or single, developing healthy relationships with other clergy and other healthy people is a must.

Dr. Mamie J. Harris Smith offers these words of wisdom: "Those of us who are in leadership need to have a safe place where we can go to be ministered to and have a time of rest. We need spiritual moms and fathers who will help us when we need counsel. If we are not careful, we will go to the sheep. We will be leading the sheep while bleeding."[5]

Forming healthy relationships with female and male clergy peers is extremely important. Women pastors frequently find themselves talking too much with their members, particularly those who have been prayer warriors or strong supporters. Since there are so few female senior pastors, clergywomen are particularly vulnerable to this dilemma. Due to a lack of peer relationships, female clergy can find themselves confiding in and venting to members or associate ministers. The old adage "Familiarity breeds contempt" is a good one to remember. It is difficult for a member or associate minister to relate to you as sister and girlfriend one day and pastor the next. Also, becoming too close to individual members can create a breeding ground for resentment, jealousy, and divisions within the church. Another unfortunate reality is that some individuals, seeing the vulnerability of the pastor, will take advantage of her revealed struggles and use them to broker deals or to wield power over her.

> **"We need spiritual moms and fathers who will help us when we need counsel. If we are not careful, we will go to the sheep. We will be leading the sheep while bleeding."**

As humans, we will naturally gravitate to those with whom we have interests in common. However, as pastors, we must be careful not to compromise the effectiveness of our ministry and position because of vulnerability. Having clergy peers—other senior pastors with whom we can relate to and share—is critical. Praying and asking the Lord for guidance and discernment in developing supportive relationships is essential. And remember this advice from one survey respondent from Maryland:

Keep a group of friends with whom you can share frustrations, struggles, highs, and lows. Don't get consumed with success. Remember that God called women to pastor as women would pastor and not as men would pastor. Many women model men's style of pastoring, which is unfortunate. Perhaps it's because we have not had enough female models, but it is imperative that we realize that we bring a unique set of gifts and compassion and empathy to the position.

If no support groups exist in your area, the Lord may be calling you to form one among local clergy. Beware of groups that do not allow new clergy or those who don't fit a certain mold to join. Remain suspect of groups where only those of the "in crowd" are welcomed. Due to this phenomenon, many clergy, male and female, go about lonely and isolated. Could the Lord be prompting you to initiate a group that would be different? Seek the Lord's direction to identify women and men who may be interested in meeting once a month or so to talk, pray, share, or be involved in certain aspects of community ministry. You may be surprised what will evolve.

The acronym **HALT** is a wonderful tool to remember: Don't allow yourself to become too hungry, too angry, too lonely, or too tired. With such a caution in mind, women must do a better job of encouraging, supporting, and being available for one another as pastors. Many single and married female pastors are walking around wounded, bleeding, and yet smiling. They are known and unknown. Some are obvious, and others can be seen only through the eyes of discernment. What are women doing to reach out to them? Are the bleeding allowing themselves to be open to support and encouragement?

Another challenge expressed by single female pastors is the expectation that because they are single, they are available to answer every whim and wish of congregants. In response to the statement, "I believe because I am single the congregation requests more of my time," approximately 52 percent of female pastors agreed. Only 21.7 percent strongly disagreed. Just because a woman does not have a husband and/or children, it does not mean she does not have a life. Single female pastors should be careful to avoid taking on excessive responsibilities because her congregants view her as free or without responsibility. Again, boundaries are crucial.

Who shall we become beyond the stained glass ceiling? It will depend upon the choices we make, the boundaries we set, the relationships we build, the perspectives we form, the attitudes we embrace, the questions we ask, and the circumstances we accept.

God Exalted over Circumstances

The experiences shared in this chapter seem overwhelming. For those who are serving in the pastoral ministry, the realities can be overwhelming unless a choice is made to focus rather upon God and God's power to reign victorious over every situation and circumstance. The writer of Psalm 57 provides a critical message that teaches the faithful how to exalt God over circumstances. The writer of Psalm 57 uses the Hebrew term *Zamar* to express praises to God through music and song. *Zamar* means "to pluck the strings of an instrument, to sing, to praise; a musical word which is largely involved with joyful expressions of music with musical instruments."

The powerful thing about this praise is that it is given during a time of deep distress. It appears that enemies sought to steal the psalmist's song, so to speak, with cruel treatment. His heart was crushed. His spirit was broken. However, the psalmist's decision to exalt God even in the midst of great suffering teaches a powerful lesson for those who are wounded.

Be exalted, O God, above the heavens;
    let your glory be over all the earth.
They spread a net for my feet—
    I was bowed down in distress.
They dug a pit in my path—
    but they have fallen into it themselves. [Selah]
My heart, O God, is steadfast,
    my heart is steadfast;
    I will sing and make music.
Awake, my soul!
    Awake, harp and lyre!
    I will awaken the dawn.
I will praise you, LORD, among the nations;
    I will sing of you among the peoples.
For great is your love, reaching to the heavens;
    your faithfulness reaches to the skies.
Be exalted, O God, above the heavens;
    let your glory be over all the earth.

                    —Psalm 57:5-11 (NIV)

In this text, it appears that the psalmist had every reason to have a crushed spirit. Enemies had stolen "his song." In verse 4 (NIV), the psalmist declared, "I am in the midst of lions; I lie among ravenous beasts—men whose teeth are spears and arrows, whose tongues are sharp swords." Have you ever experienced the pain of being attacked by mean-spirited people? Not necessarily physically attacked, but having your character attacked, your name dragged through the mud, your motives questioned, and your every move considered suspect? If you have, then you can relate to the psalmist.

The pain inflicted by the tongue sometimes lasts years longer than any bruise caused by a physical punch. All too many of us as pastors have known the feeling of someone waiting to pounce on us with cruel words or with a plot to get us removed from the pulpit. That sense of foreboding can break even a strong woman's spirit and make her feel sick. The psalmist said that such enemies seem to be ravenous beasts. Verbal attacks can produce some serious pain. They can leave us, as they did the psalmist, without a song—but not for long! Something happened within the psalmist. The Hebrew word that marked this transition was *Zamar*.

The psalmist stepped over the pain of attacks and began to pluck the strings of his heart, declaring, "Be exalted, O God, above the heavens; let your glory be over all the earth." Even though our enemies may plot against us, they may be caught in their own traps. No wonder the Scripture says next, "Selah," a term that is not to be spoken but is an instruction to pause and think about what has just been said.

We may say with the psalmist, "They spread a net for my feet, I was bowed down in distress, they dug a pit in my path, but they have fallen into it themselves" (v. 6). And then, we must also stop and think about what God has done and declare, "My heart is steadfast, O God, my heart is steadfast; I will sing and make music" (v. 7).

Women pastors, think about God's deliverance, God's protection, God's exaltation, and God's removal of the onslaught of the enemies' attacks against you. Stop and think about those who tried to kill your spirit, crush your dreams, steal your joy, scandalize your name, and then shout, "Zamar!" Realize that you still have a song.

We've seen our pastor matriarchs declare with strength, faith, and determination, "My heart is steadfast, O God, my heart is steadfast. I will sing and make music." Make up your mind to sing your song! Much in life will try to steal your song. Much in life will threaten to break your spirit, to crush your dreams, to laugh at your vision, to press down your enthusiasm, but you've got to declare with the women preachers and pastors of old, "Zamar! I will sing and make music."

No matter who tried to tell these women that they could not preach, that they could not pastor, that God would not use them in that way, they kept on singing, kept on shouting, kept on serving, kept on praising, kept on proclaiming, kept on preaching, kept on teaching, kept on climbing, kept on marching up the King's highway. They were determined to exalt God over their circumstances. Even though they were denied access to physical pulpits, God used them to pastor many and to kick open doors that we have begun to walk through.

Women of God, sing your song. Exalt God in your life. Sing your song. Cast down the demons of depression. Exalt God in your life. Proclaim God's glory unto yourself. Exalt God in your life. Refuse to accept a report of defeat. The prophet Isaiah raised the question, "Whose report will you believe?" Determine to believe the report of the Lord.

God's steadfast love will keep you. Sing your song. Don't allow the hardships of ministry to prevent you from plucking your heart strings. Shout, "Zamar" and proclaim, "Be exalted, O God, above the heavens. Let your glory be over all of the earth and over all of my life."

Notes

1. Christine A. Smith, interview with Jacquelyn Ragin Olds, December 8, 2011, Cleveland, Ohio.

2. Kathleen Bostrom, "Effective Clergy Couples," *The Christian Ministry,* May–June 1997, 29–31.

3. Colette M. Jenkins, "Clergy Couples Strive to Balance Marriage and Ministry," *Akron Beacon Journal,* August 20, 2011, www.ohio.com/news/local/clergy-couples-strive-to-balance-marriage-and-ministry-1.230597 (accessed November 23, 2012).

4. Wren Miller, "Confessions of a Single, Female Pastor," *Marie Claire*, February 9, 2011, www.marieclaire.com/sex-love/relation-ship-issues/female-pastor-love-life (accessed November 23, 2012).

5. Christine A. Smith, interview with Mamie J. Harris Smith, November 2011, Griffin, Georgia.

CHAPTER 7

What Will We Need to Press On?

Don't push your way to the front; don't sweet-talk your way to the top. Put yourself aside, and help others get ahead. Don't be obsessed with getting your own advantage. Forget yourselves long enough to lend a helping hand. (Philippians 2:3-4, The Message)

While it is hard to believe that women still have to break through stained glass ceilings, the reality yet exists. So the question remains, What *do* we need to keep pressing forward? Included in the recommendations are adequate compensation, grants and funding for the practical support of women in ministry, the education of churches by denominations on the validity of female pastors, and insights from advocates on how to provide greater support to women in ministry.

Adequate Compensation

One of the greatest challenges that many female pastors face is the lack of financial resources. Some people may argue that money is not a major issue or factor. However, it cannot be underestimated. Women must break free from the habit of denying the need for financial support. Women in ministry have publicly decried the need for funding but privately expressed their financial struggles. Although some congregations have endowments that keep them going, many if not most of the churches where women are called do not. Because their membership is largely the elderly, the members give out of their fixed incomes. Smaller congregations are typically comprised of the very elderly and the very young, neither of whom have substantial income to share.

If the church building is an older structure, it most probably has been severely neglected and needs repairs. Leaking roofs, molding carpet, and broken water heaters are not uncommon. Frequently, the pastor uses her own resources to assist in paying for repairs, buying supplies, and providing funding to promote special events and programs. So much time and energy are spent on attempting to keep the ministry afloat that her energy and morale can become depleted. Building up the church ends up on the back burner; putting out fires becomes the focus.

Single female pastors, particularly if they have children, can have a major dilemma. Out of necessity, many are bi-vocational, struggling to pay for family needs or children in college. Even those without children find themselves needing to secure additional employment because the pay is low and sometimes unstable, and benefits may or may not be an option. A married female pastor may not face the same depth of financial struggle as a single pastor if she has the financial support of her husband. He may carry the medical benefits for the family, and thus, lack of benefits from the church may not be a problem. However, if her pay is lowered due to decreased church giving, the stability of the two-income household can be devastated. She too may be forced to obtain another job to make ends meet. A husband in this predicament may become frustrated and resentful toward the church, and the marriage may begin to suffer.

It is not uncommon for a female pastor to be faced with the church making a choice of paying the heating bill or paying her salary. If she demands her pay, the building is cold and the people are bewildered. If she allows her salary to be used to pay bills, the church becomes indifferent, and a pattern may begin to be established. With her faith challenged, her vision blurred, her motivation drained, her wonderful ideas tabled, she fights against despondency. She presses on, desperately seeking resources while praying her way through. She is still preacher, teacher, and encourager in chief. She is still called to the bedside of the sick, sought after by troubled souls needing a word of counsel or inspiration, asked to attend the juvenile court hearing, and expected to tell the lost about salvation. Her mind tells her, "Girl, you are crazy!" The bill collector tells her, "That partial payment you made is not sufficient." Her heart tells her, "You are a pastor—trust God!"

One might ask, "Why in the world would anybody remain in such a dire predicament?" The short answer is, "The call." The question, however, for the church, denominational leaders, and advocates of female clergy is, "Can you do better?" The heavens resound, "Yes, you can!" In order to press on, there needs to be an acknowledgment that the process is broken in order to move forward with the business of making repairs. Bulletin inserts and special DVDs about women in ministry on a particular Sunday annually is a start; however, things of greater depth and with further reach are needed.

Financial Support

Grants and funds for the practical support of women in ministry need to be established. Just as monies have been made available for sabbaticals, support groups (e.g., Together in Ministry Groups), and special ministry projects, it is necessary to develop a strategic plan for creating financial support for women in ministry. While it is hoped that more women will have the opportunity to serve in larger, more financially stable congregations, many will not. Those interested in advocating for women in ministry must consider creating avenues of support for those who pastor smaller congregations.

It is not enough to say that women need to develop strategic plans and pursue grant opportunities on their own. Female pastors need advocates to work to make inroads where few exist. Advocates can host roundtable discussions that include clergywomen and identify specific areas in which financial support is needed. Frequently, grant requests for the practical support of ministry are denied. Denominational leaders can help to make the case for the validity and critical nature of such requests. Smaller congregations also deserve quality leaders. Women who feel called to serve such congregations need assistance to ensure stable, competitive pay and resources to assist with the maintenance of the physical plant. Focus groups of female pastors can be gathered to collect data, share testimonies, and cast visions for what is required to survive and thrive in a small, economically depressed church. Denominational leaders can use the information obtained to justify specific funding for practical ministry needs. This can cultivate supportive structures and increase the potential for donors or grantors to provide financial assistance. Including a category to support female pastors through planned giving discussions with individuals and congregations can also help to accomplish this goal. Advocates can approach philanthropic entities such as the Lilly Foundation, the Ford Foundation, and others with a comprehensive plan to aid women in ministry. A grant requesting major funding for the practical support of female pastors may include the following.

Salary/benefit support for new pastors. Salary support would be up to half of the annual salary. For example, if the salary is

$45,000, the church may be able to pay only $25,000. The national grant program would provide support by paying the other $20,000 and a portion of the pastor's retirement and medical benefits for the first five years of her pastorate.

Building fund support for smaller, female-led congregations. Funds for major repairs could be made up to a certain amount.

Assistance with outreach programs. Special resources (financial, program resources, national staff) could be available for female pastors to draw upon to assist in rebuilding and further developing once-dying ministries.

If female pastors could receive these kinds of practical support, accepting a call to a small, fractured, dying congregation might be more workable and certainly a blessing for her health and well-being.

Educating Churches on the Validity of Female Pastors

The next recommendation is advocacy from denominations to educate churches on the validity of female pastors so that congregations look past gender and look at qualifications. In general, the tide appears to be shifting toward genuine support for women in ministry. Many Protestant denominations are making strides toward opening the door for female clergy to serve in historically male-dominated positions. However, large percentages of women still lag behind men in senior pastor roles.

An excellent example of advocacy for women pastors is a United Methodist strategic plan entitled "Advocate, Monitor, Change Agent: Accomplishing the Work of the Conference Commission on the Status and Role of Women."[1] The United Methodists used this plan to review the trends of women in ministry, identify their core values and beliefs regarding the role of women in ministry, explore the hindrances to women's advancement, and develop and implement specific plans to increase support for women pastors. This same plan used concrete examples of how the United Methodist conferences could work together to open doors for women to become pastors in healthy, thriving congregations.

Regarding the view, "the future may show a female-dominated clergy in these denominations." In 1979, Dr. Letty M. Russell, associate professor of theology at Yale University Divinity School, stated:

> The entrance of large numbers of women into ordained ministry may cause it to become a "female profession" like nursing or primary school teaching. Sexism causes work done by women to be devalued in society; when large numbers of them enter a field, the men tend to leave; prestige and salaries drop. If this prejudice continues, it may cause ordained ministry, which is already associated with the private sphere and with feminine cultural characteristics of being loving and kind, to become not only "feminized" but also "female." Clerical ministry as a female profession is by no means the only alternate scenario, but it is important to notice the trends pointing in this direction in order to work for a more balanced professional ministry that neither keeps women out because of sexism nor turns over jobs to women because of sexism, but recognizes the gifts of both women and men in a partnership of ministry.[2]

It is unfortunate that the words ring true in this century as well. As increasing numbers of women enter seminary and subsequently the church, a feminization of the pastorate may lead to the trends spoken of by Dr. Russell. Therefore, every effort must be made to keep a balance between men and women regarding salary being commensurate with education and experience, and creating greater opportunities for women to be called to stable ministry settings.

So then, what does true advocacy look like? Is it merely placing women in leadership roles that men don't want? Is it creating an environment where women dominate the field and men flee? How do advocates foster an environment where the gifts of men and women are equally valued and appropriately matched with ministry venues?

As mentioned earlier, the United Methodist General Commission on the Status and Role of Women offers some first steps. Excerpts from their strategies are listed below.

Examples of advocacy

■ Host listening sessions for seminary women and report what they hear.
■ Work with groups within the denomination to orient new women members to the annual conference and delegates to general and jurisdictional conferences.
■ Work with Religion & Race to hear and report concerns of racial-ethnic clergywomen.
■ Review conference budgets for inclusion of women-friendly initiatives and women's leadership, and push for greater representation.

What to monitor

■ Women as leaders in nontraditional vs. more traditional roles; men's participation in advocacy for women.
■ New women and girls being recruited and mentored into leadership positions.
■ Number of women and men in unofficial as well as official decision-making roles.
■ Systematic exclusion of so-called troublemakers, especially women and people of color.

Be a change agent

■ Speak truth to power, even when it is not popular, in order to bring the church into full and faithful witness for Christ.[3]

Those who are in positions of power have to help in making the case for supporting women in ministry. Leaders in general and empowering men in particular can be effective in helping to open doors for female pastors. Male clergy and denominational leaders who have encouraged and supported women in word but then followed up their words with action have important views and strategies to share.

Recommendations from Supportive Male Clergy

As is true with any major movement or paradigm shift, those who are trying to enter a door or break through a barrier need assistance from those already on the other side. For example, in order for the Underground Railroad to work, there had to be free individuals who were willing to allow their homes to be secret places of refuge along the way. In order for the civil rights movement to be effective, there had to be individuals who would march, provide legal assistance, vote, and sign legislation into law in order for equal rights to become a reality.

In like manner, women seeking to gain entrance or additional access to the ministry and the pastorate need male advocates who will give women opportunities to be licensed and ordained, to preach, and to be recommended as successors to their pastorates.

Following are the words of several supportive male clergy. Each agreed to answer a series of questions regarding advocacy for women in ministry. The interviews conducted with Drs. Lacy and Moss and Bishop Finney were done with me in person. The interviews with Drs. Rolfs-Massaglia and Norwood were form-based and sent in via e-mail.

Support for Female Clergy
CS: In word and deed, you have demonstrated strong support for female clergy. What factors influenced your stance?

Rev. Dr. Martin Rolfs-Massaglia, Senior Pastor, First Baptist Church of Greater Cleveland. While not directly involved with the call of his successor, Dr. Rolfs-Massaglia creatively and deliberately laid the groundwork for his former congregation, Royersford Baptist Church in Royersford, Pennsylvania, to call a woman, Rev. Karen Selig, as their senior pastor upon his departure (Form Interview, January 31, 2012).

> This has long been an issue of great importance to me, and I've tried in various ways to be a strong advocate of women in ministry. Not only is it clear that Jesus had women disciples; it is very clear that women held leadership in the church described by Paul. Beyond that I have just known too, too many women who have clearly been called into pastoral ministry and who have the gifts necessary to function in the pastoral role.

Bishop Benjamin G. Finney, Pastor, Omega Baptist Church, East Cleveland, Ohio. As founder of Omega Baptist Church (1977), Bishop Finney came to embrace the call of his daughter, Rev. Patrice Finney, to the ministry only after being convicted by the Holy Spirit. Years later he is laying the groundwork for her to become his successor upon retirement (Interview, January 11, 2012, Cleveland, Ohio).

> My mindset was that no woman should be in the pulpit to preach. That is what I had been taught. God taught me that there is neither male nor female in Christ. I learned that God could use a woman as well as men. Esther, Ruth, Rahab were all used by God. God has used women all through the Scripture.
>
> My daughter attended a conference for women in ministry. When she came back, I saw the spirit of the Lord

upon her. She did not tell me that she was called to preach, but I saw the Lord's hand upon her. Although I could see the spirit of the Lord upon her, what I was seeing went against everything that I'd ever been taught.

The Lord was putting upon my heart that he had summoned her to preach the gospel. At first, I'd hardened my heart like Pharaoh. But the Lord softened my heart, and I yielded. Many gifts came forth after my acceptance of her gift.

Rev. Dr. Cleopatrick Lacy, Pastor, Mount Zion Baptist Church, Griffin, Georgia. Dr. Lacy served as instructor for homiletics, missiology, and Baptist polity at the Interdenominational Theological Center in Atlanta, Georgia, for more than sixteen years. In his role as professor and pastor, he touched the lives of many seminary students in general and took under his wing several adopted daughters in particular, allowing them to serve as student interns with his congregation (Interview, February 4, 2012, Griffin, Georgia).

> Early on in my life and in my family as a child, I had a cousin we called "cousin Connie." She was a Pentecostal/Holiness preacher. She preached in the community and among our family. I remember her coming by the house. We liked her, loved her, and were taught to love her. She may not have had a church building, but she had a storefront or preached out of her house. We were taught to respect her and her ministry. That was my first experience knowing about women in ministry.
>
> As time passed, I received my call into the ministry and went off to college. On the college campus, women were a part of the religious organizations. As young adults, we learned to respect women serving in the ministry. They may not have been ordained, but they participated and led chapel services.

When I went to seminary I had the opportunity to be classmates with then-students Dr. Katie Cannon and Dr. Jaquelyn Grant. Having them as classmates caused us to develop an even deeper respect for women in ministry. I was also greatly influenced to respect the role of women in ministry as I observed my wife, Portia Lacy, as she studied Christian education in seminary. When we moved to Houston, Texas, and attended Wheeler Avenue Baptist Church, we experienced a female associate minister who led noonday service. My pastor, Bill Lawson, advocated for women in the ministry. It was no hardship to accept her in the ministry.

I must say that the experience that most affected my acceptance of women in ministry was the opportunity I was given to preach the ordination service for a local female minister (now senior pastor of her own church), Mamie Harris. My overt support of women in ministry came along when Rev. Christine Small came to seminary and I adopted her as a seminary student.

Rev. Dr. Monte Norwood, Senior Pastor, Bible Way Ministries International, Atlanta, Georgia. Dr. Norwood was directly involved with nurturing, teaching, encouraging, and ultimately recommending his successor, Rev. Michele Humphrey, to become senior pastor of his former congregation, Imani United Church of Christ in Euclid, Ohio, upon his departure (Form Interview, December 19, 2011).

Though raised in the Deep South in a strongly patriarchal and sexist culture in general, and church culture in particular, it honestly never occurred to me that God could not and would not call a woman and use her in ministry. Though I largely had no examples of female clergy growing up in

Atlanta, Georgia, I had the heritage that my paternal grandmother was one of three praying women who led a house-to-house prayer meeting in the community and who became responsible for founding the church that I grew up in and that my father came to serve as pastor for forty-four years. Further, in retrospect, while the church in which I was reared strongly taught, at that time and throughout my early and formative years, that women were not called by God and could not serve in ministry, I was exposed to and aware of very strong women with ministry gifts who had to speak and not preach—though it seemed to me the same thing—from the floor of the sanctuary rather than the pulpit. They were often called and referred to as either a missionary or an evangelist. In this tradition, my mother and maternal grandmother were very prominent figures in my life as prayer warriors, teachers, speakers, and as strong a spiritual presence in my life as any male I ever knew or experienced.

I have always believed, accepted, and sought to practice the conviction that God can call and use whomever God chooses, whether female or male without limitation. I believe in, as 1 Peter 2:9 states, the priesthood of all believers, female and male. I believe, as Galatians 3:28 states, that in Christ there is no male and female. Further, I just believe that -isms in this world—including sexism, chauvinism, and misogynistic thinking—in a world tainted by the fall in the Garden of Eden, introducing sin into the world and tainting creation, is what sin caused and not at all what God intended. So, as a member of a racial ethnic minority in the United States, I am painfully aware of prejudice, discrimination, and racism that seek to diminish who I am and whose I am and have therefore, because of this, embraced the truth and inclusive models in Scripture, consciously chosen to fully, thoroughly, and forcefully support female clergy and women serving in any and every ministry capacity possible.

Rev. Dr. Otis Moss Jr., Pastor Emeritus, Olivet Institutional Baptist Church, Cleveland, Ohio. Dr. Moss facilitated the licensure and ordination of the first female minister, Rev. Dr. Margaret J. Mitchell, at a major African American congregation in the greater Cleveland area. Upon his retirement, he was also instrumental in having her named interim pastor. Furthermore, he laid the groundwork for the historic Olivet Institutional Baptist Church to have among its four final candidates for the pastorate a woman, Rev. Christine A. Smith (the author of this book). Although I did not obtain the pastorate there, I became the first female associate of the congregation to become a senior pastor of another established congregation in the greater Cleveland area (Interview, February 6, 2012, Cleveland, Ohio).

> One, I think if I could term it so, a paradigm shift in my own being started with seminary, but it was not pushed. The concept was there, just by the presence of female faculty as well as the openness of my professors. But as open as they were, their openness was in academia, not necessarily in church and community. Second, the whole experience in the civil rights movement lifted up not only the contradictions in our society and in our nation but also the contradictions in our personal lives.
>
> Next to that was grappling with the whole concept of nonviolence as expressed and lived out through the unconditional love of Jesus Christ. When you think deeply and sincerely and with devotion to these ideals and concepts, you have to constantly look at your own being and context and raise questions with yourself if you are to grow in grace.

So when I came to the moment (and I would say it was coming no matter where I might have been) in Olivet when a person acknowledged her call to ministry, I had to raise the question, first privately, "Lord, what would thou have me to do?" And the answer was obvious: "You've got to welcome this individual into the ministry under your administration, not based on gender but based on the spirit of Christ and all that you have been proclaiming."

Then the challenge—how do we introduce what to some would be considered radical and revolutionary into a relatively traditional congregation? A congregation populated by women and dominated by men. And that is a serious kind of reality to deal with. So, without announcing it, I started to work seeking to lift the congregation to another level.

I did not come with a prepared strategic plan, but wherever I was, in a prayer meeting, Sunday school class, a sermon, or just an informal conversation, I started building the concept of "all" without even announcing what I was doing. And then, when I felt that we had laid the foundation sufficiently, I made the move. For some, it was not soon enough, and for some it was way too soon. But it was done in such a way, by the grace of God, that there was full acceptance. And those who did not accept it did not challenge it. Once the door was open, nobody had anything against me or the minister. They had no logical legs upon which to stand. Once the door was open, nobody could shut it, and it grew from that point on.

I still don't know what might have been the quiet disapprovals—I know about the community—but not in the congregation. Once we opened the door, I thought it was also important to work with female ministers or candidates to help them to wear the shield of faith in the wider community. Because I knew that they would face all kind of barriers—rejections, and maybe occasional insults from other pastors and laity, some out of a deep-seated dogmatic position, and some out of threat or perceived threats in their own ministries and leadership.

CS: Other than leaving her denomination (often the case for Baptist women), what can a woman do to increase the likelihood of being called to a pastorate?

Rev. Dr. Martin Rolfs-Massaglia

Women need to seek and nurture relationships with those who are in the position of helping churches find pastors: area ministers and executive ministers, lay leaders of judicatories, prominent pastors in their area. Women need preaching and pastoral exposure. Serving in interim ministry has provided that for some women. As a strong advocate for women in ministry, when I brought substitute preachers to the pulpit in my last church I worked hard to find women.

Bishop Benjamin G. Finney

A woman first of all has to prove herself to be ordained and approved of God. She must make full manifestation of her calling. She must walk circumspectly in the world. She has to be a preacher. She has to be able to reach people. It would be best for her to come up under someone's tutelage who would endorse her. Your gift will make room for you.

Rev. Dr. Cleopatrick Lacy

She should begin talking to other ministers who are getting ready to retire, seek to nurture a relationship with them.

Possibly, one might be willing to take her under his [or her] wing and recommend her as a successor. Consider asking a male pastor to recommend her to a pulpit committee. She needs to be theologically trained.

Rev. Dr. Monte Norwood

In my experience, being open and willing to leave her denomination is often the fateful choice of last resort. Seeking dual standing (ordination, alliance, and/or whatever the particulars of the denomination's polity is applying to serve its congregations) may be a creative option. Further, she can seek a sensitive, enlightened, open, and nurturing pastor, congregation, and church setting that will support her and be open either to calling her or recommending her to a pastorate.

Rev. Dr. Otis Moss Jr.

Bonding with other women and men who offer fellowship, dialogue, and from time to time take opportunities to participate and grow in ministry. Engage or allow yourself to be engaged in endeavors beyond just the local church. Seek a definition of ministry that is larger than just the pastorate. When another pastor was called to a church he gave an interesting story. His father said to him, "Thank God, you are finally entering the ministry!" Had been to seminary, graduated as a scholar, was president of a school, but he was not considered to be doing ministry until he was called to pastor. These were his parents. Historically, among black Baptists, our definition of ministry has long been restricted to being a senior pastor. A very important, consecrated calling, but not the alpha and omega of ministry.

Dr. Mordecai Johnson was called from the pastorate of First Baptist West Virginia to the presidency of Howard

University. Despite great opposition from elite scholars among the faculty, he brought the law school from an unaccredited night school to an accredited, first-class law school that went on to graduate Thurgood Marshall and became the seat of producing constitutional lawyers and scholars that eventually brought us the Supreme Court decision of 1954, *Brown v. Board of Education.*

Howard University produced many of the best leaders, lawyers and writers this nation has known. Thurgood Marshall, Vernon Jordan and Toni Morrison are all graduates of Howard University. Here we are talking about the leadership of a black Baptist pastor who left the pastorate and became a university dean (who incidentally was kicked out of college for one semester for playing cards). The pastoral ministry is a great calling, but it is not the only assignment that God gives us.

It might be in some instances that you will have to cross denominational lines. In some instances God blesses us to initiate a ministry. There are other ways of breaking the ceiling. Sometimes it will not be broken with the church structure as we know it. So we have to be prepared to explore or be open to all of those avenues.

Assistance in Opening Doors

CS: In your opinion, what can advocates of female clergy do to assist in opening doors for women to become senior pastors?

Rev. Dr. Martin Rolfs-Massaglia

Invite them to preach in their churches; forward their names to pulpit committees; speak to area or regional executives about them; help them find opportunities to put their pastoral gifts on display.

Bishop Benjamin G. Finney

Fathers have to recommend their daughters (biological or in the ministry). Pastors should document their support for a woman to become the pastor. The pastor needs to prepare the church. Put it in writing before you leave.

Rev. Dr. Cleopatrick Lacy

Adopt female seminarians to work with them as associates. Assist them in their ministerial development. Reach out to other male and female pastors and colleagues and ask them to offer preaching opportunities to female clergy on major events like revivals, community services, and Sunday worship when they are out of the pulpit. When the opportunity comes, recommend them to church pulpit committees.

Rev. Dr. Monte Norwood

Be sensitive, strategic, vocal, supportive, aware, and decisive; network, build relationships, respond to concerns, enlighten, recommend, and urge dialogue and openness in every possible and appropriate setting for the regular and consistent consideration and call of women as senior pastors.

Rev. Dr. Otis Moss Jr.

We must continue to advocate and demonstrate support in our own context through faith, love, and action. We have to continue to teach, write, motivate, and look constantly for ways to explore avenues and opportunities to intentionally put women in places of leadership, commensurate with their calling and ability. It is amazing how we can put unqualified males in certain positions and come up with a super-qualified female and declare, "not yet." Sexism and racism are almost the omnipotent. But remember, "almost." I see this as a generational struggle, not the struggle of the decade, but generational.

Encouragement

CS: What words of encouragement would you share with women who feel called to the pastorate but lack opportunity?

Rev. Dr. Martin Rolfs-Massaglia

Honestly, I don't know what to say to women who feel called to the pastorate. I'm appalled that the church in general, and particularly among Baptists, is SO far behind on this issue. I have told women to understand themselves as pioneers. Whatever trails they blaze, interim pastor, pastor, associate pastor . . . they are paving the way for a new generation.

Bishop Benjamin G. Finney

Continue in Christ. Do not be discouraged. David encouraged himself. You've got to encourage yourself to remain on the battlefield. It's hard because of the old boys' club.

Rev. Dr. Cleopatrick Lacy

Know that they have been called. If you know you are called by God, then you won't become discouraged because of the lack of opportunity. Be sure of your calling and go to school, because education will open opportunities for you. Accept the little assignments that are given to you, teaching Sunday school, Bible study, and so on. Sometimes you are being tested to do the little things before being invited to the pulpit. If you are not pastoring, go and worship and support the pastor in another church. Go to church. Show up to worship. That will create opportunities for you. Do what you are asked to do. Follow instructions.

Rev. Dr. Monte Norwood

Know yourself. Know your God. Know your call. Know that God has given you powerful promises including God's invitation for you to "ask, seek, and knock"—and God's promise to respond (Matthew 7:7-11). God has also promised to do exceeding and abundantly above all we can ask or think (Ephesians 3:20-21). What a promise! The challenge, of course, is God's timetable and methodology in responding. As with many areas of our lives and the human condition, perhaps God mixes the conundrum of the search, the waiting, and answering the prayer for pastoral opportunities with the opportunity to learn greater patience and to experience fulfillment along the journey (Isaiah 40:31; Isaiah 55:8-9; Galatians 5:25). The best encouragement I can give is never, never, ever give up! As long as you have a pulse—God has a purpose! God's gifting and calling in your life will make room for their expression for God's glory.

"As long as you have a pulse— God has a purpose!"

Rev. Dr. Otis Moss Jr.

Never give up. Do not allow the zeal for the pastorate to cause you to become dispirited or frustrated when opportunities are blocked. We can never let up or give up no matter how politicized the process might become or how reinforced the ceiling might appear to be—it is not impenetrable.

What powerful expressions of support, advocacy, and instructions on behalf of and for female pastors! In chapter 8, "A Final

Word for Churches and Denominational Leaders," additional guidance from these empowering advocates will be given.

Several recommendations for what female pastors need to press on, such as adequate compensations, education for churches on the validity of female pastors, and advocacy, have been addressed. The next sections provide additional suggestions for clergywomen.

Create a Beloved Community

I have heard it said that we need to be the beloved community that we talk about. The idea of the beloved community as advanced by the late Rev. Dr. Martin Luther King Jr. was a vision for integration that surpassed legislative procedures of desegregation and embraced true interrelatedness. While Dr. King was referring to racial integration, the concept is also appropriate for bringing about equality and integration of women into the pastoral ministry.

In order to press on, the need is for more than rules and regulations that may begin the process but will not be transformative in the long run. What is needed is a change of heart and attitude through love. Kenneth L. Smith and Ira G. Zepp Jr. suggest, "Whereas desegregation can be brought about by laws, integration requires a change in attitudes. It involves personal and social relationships that are created by love—and these cannot be legislated."[4]

As advocates work to create broader opportunities for women to become senior pastors, consideration must be given to the most effective ways to bridge the gap between functional togetherness and oneness. Women must not be merely thrust into positions, but rather, time must be taken to cultivate an appreciation of the value they bring to the ministry. Through education (scriptural teachings and social awareness of the leadership roles women have held historically), through example (placing women in leadership roles based upon their gifts and talents), and through opportunity (calling upon women to preach, teach, pray, read Scripture, preside at business meetings, and be part of decision making), perceptions will begin to change and a willingness to accept women as pastors will ultimately increase.

To further expand upon King's concept of the beloved community, Smith and Zepp state:

> Behind King's conception of the Beloved Community lay his assumption that human existence is social in nature. "The solidarity of the human family" is a phrase he frequently used to express this idea. . . . This was a way of affirming that reality is made up of structures that form an interrelated whole; in other words, that human beings are dependent upon each other. Whatever a person is or possesses he owes to others who have preceded him.[5]

If we are to be the beloved community, we must follow the Golden Rule, "Do unto others as you would have them do unto you." Women and men in the ministry must not simply tolerate one another, but out of a common purpose they must strive to open doors of opportunity where padlocks exist. Love must not cover but transform attitudes of chauvinism, sexism, separatism, and elitism to attitudes of equality, togetherness, mutual support, and lifting as we climb.

Women Must Continue to Help Women

Women must continue to help women though and beyond the stained glass ceiling. Sister Mary Luke Jones of Our Lady of Grace Monastery in Indiana provides several suggestions for how clergy women can encourage one another.[6] Her suggestions flow from

Women Touched by Grace, a spiritual renewal program that brought together female Catholic religious and Protestant clergywomen:

> Catholic women are denied ordination, so we chose to reach out to Protestant clergywomen, for a number of reasons. First, we like women. We think they can change the world. Second, we honor women for the role they play in family, church and society. Third, we value women because for too long they have been relegated to second place. And fourth, half of the brain power in our world lies in the heads of its women. If we do not mine it, it is at our own peril.[7]

Among the lessons are the need for community, the companionship of other women, and especially prayer. Establishing a "rhythm of prayer" through the recitation of the psalms, studying the Scriptures, and spending time in meditation will draw us into a deep place of intimacy with God. However, Sister Mary Luke explains, the variety of roles female pastors are forced to play as "being a stray dog at a whistler's convention" deteriorate the time to refresh and renew a clergywoman's spirit and prayer life.[8]

Our quest to advance beyond the stained glass ceiling in greater numbers will meet with success only if we strengthen our support as women for one another. We must look beyond our differences and focus rather upon our commonalities. We must strive to have more than cosmetic unity and togetherness and seek to develop greater depths of camaraderie.

Things We Can Learn from the Brethren

"Wisdom is the principal thing; therefore get wisdom: and with all thy getting get understanding" (Proverbs 4:7, KJV). The term "principal" means "most important, consequential, or influential:

chief." As a child, I was taught to remember the difference between "principal" and "principle" (a rule or code of conduct) by thinking of the school director or leader as our "pal." With that distinction in mind, as well as the childhood imagery of a pal, Proverbs 4:7 can take on an interesting meaning: Seeking wisdom should be a top priority in our lives. We should make wisdom our best friend. Wisdom challenges us to consider the broader scope of things and make decisions that are good, not only for the moment but also for the long haul. I would like to suggest that women clergy could learn some things from male clergy that will benefit us over time.

The other day I heard a clergywoman say, "Men can argue all morning long in the board room but go out to the golf course together in the afternoon." She was suggesting that in general, men are adept at separating business from personal relationships, net-working, and camaraderie. Of course, we have seen men ostracize one another, be cutthroat, and have their own cliques and clans in business meetings, but we have also observed their ability to make connections, look for who has certain areas of expertise and tap into their reservoir of resources, come together to get a job done, and then go out together and take in a sports event.

What, in wisdom, can we learn from their behaviors?

■ *Separate personal issues from business.* Even if you don't like the way she acts or dresses, is there something you can learn from her? Is there any area in which you could collaborate?

■ *Learn how to disagree and let it go.* So often our boardroom dis-agreements turn into long-term "I can't stand her!" As a result, we miss opportunities to make connections, listen and learn, consider another person's point of view, and grow as Christians.

■ *Learn the benefits of playing well together.* Women miss so many chances to network and experience open doors and to open doors for others, lifting as we climb. Frequently we allow our differences, jealousies, fears, and insecurities to hinder the power and blessing of joining forces together with other women.

In wisdom, let's learn. The next time you find yourself in a room full of men with one or two sisters scattered in the mix, take time to introduce yourself to them. Take time to talk to them about their work, their lives, and the ministries in which they serve. Avoid the temptation to hang out only with the boys. Even if, due to the unfortunate patterns of behaviors common to the few who make it into the circle, the women appear cold, disinterested, disconnected, and even disrespectful, take the challenge to push past all of that and be the standard bearer.

In the spirit of wisdom, show other sisters how to affirm, encourage, lift, support, include, understand, and advocate for other women. Even if you are misunderstood, rejected, given the cold shoulder, or negatively spoken of, push forward. Your light, your example, your bold spirit, your love for the Lord and the "sisteren" will ultimately break down barriers, create opportunities, and develop new and productive patterns for women to follow. We are better together. In wisdom, let's learn and march on!

Notes

1. "Advocate, Monitor, Change Agent: Accomplishing the Work of the Conference Commission on the Status and Role of Women," www.gcrsw.org (accessed November 24, 2012).

2. Letty M. Russell, "Clerical Ministry as a Female Profession," in "Women Clergy: How Their Presence Is Changing the Church," a symposium, *Christian Century,* February 7–14, 1979, 122, http://www.religion-online.org/showarticle.asp?title=1207 (accessed November 24, 2012).

3. "Advocate, Monitor, Change Agent." To read more of this presentation on advocacy for women in ministry, visit www.gcrsw.org and type into the search box, "Accomplishing the

work of the Conference Commission on the Status and Role of Women."

4. Kenneth L. Smith and Ira G. Zepp Jr., "Martin Luther King's Vision of the Beloved Community," adapted from *Search for the Beloved Community: The Thinking of Martin Luther King Jr.* (Valley Forge, PA: Judson Press, 1974), in *Christian Century,* April 3, 1974, 361–63, http://www.religion-online.org/show article. asp ?title=1603 (accessed November 24, 2012).

5. Smith and Zepp, "Martin Luther King's Vision of the Beloved Community."

6. Sister Mary Luke Jones, "The Wisdom of Women," *Faith and Leadership,* June 15, 2010, http://www.faithandleadership.com/content/the-wisdom-women (accessed November 24, 2012).

7. Jones, "The Wisdom of Women."

8. Jones, "The Wisdom of Women."

CHAPTER 8

A Final Word for Churches
and Denominational Leaders

I commend to you our sister Phoebe, a servant of the church in Cenchrea. I ask you to receive her in the Lord in a way worthy of the saints and to give her any help she may need from you, for she has been a great help to many people, including me. (Romans 16:1-2, NIV)

Romans 16 may be one of the most extensive passages of Scripture that validates the ministry of women in the New Testament church. Although the apostle Paul's words have been used to deny women roles as pastors, in Romans 16 Paul offered a model of how today's advocates can "commend" women, encouraging others to value their abilities to lead congregations. In this passage, Paul publicly recognized the contributions of women along with men. His casual mention of their names suggests that their ministry was common. Paul emphasized their work, their value, and the importance of their ministry. In so doing, he strongly validated their roles as ministers. Romans 16:3-15 (NIV) clearly illustrates this point. The names of women endorsed by Paul are in bold type.

> Greet **Priscilla** and Aquila, my fellow workers in Christ Jesus. They risked their lives for me. Not only I but all the

churches of the Gentiles are grateful to them. Greet also the church that meets at their house.

Greet my dear friend Epenetus, who was the first convert to Christ in the province of Asia. Greet **Mary**, who worked very hard for you. Greet Andronicus and **Junias**, my relatives who have been in prison with me. They are outstanding among the apostles, and they were in Christ before I was. Greet Ampliatus, whom I love in the Lord. Greet Urbanus, our fellow worker in Christ, and my dear friend Stachys. Greet Apelles, tested and approved in Christ. Greet those who belong to the household of Aristobulus. Greet Herodion, my relative. Greet those in the household of Narcissus who are in the Lord.

Greet **Tryphena** and **Tryphosa**, those women who work hard in the Lord. Greet my dear friend **Persis**, another woman who has worked very hard in the Lord. Greet Rufus, chosen in the Lord, and **his mother**, who has been a mother to me, too. Greet Asyncritus, Phlegon, Hermes, Patrobas, Hermas and the brothers with them. Greet Philologus, **Julia**, Nereus and **his sister**, and Olympas and all the saints with them.

Today's advocates can glean much from Paul's example as they strive to educate the twenty-first-century church regarding female clergy.

At the beginning of this book, emphasis was given to surveys and trends that reflect realities for clergywomen:

Barriers exist—true. One cannot ignore them—also true. But equally true is the observation that identifying and coping with barriers is not what predicts success or failure at breaking into the supply of jobs. Then what does predict success? The best predictor of success in placement is a realistic placement strategy that takes advantage of structures that link candidates with churches.[1]

How can women and their advocates "take advantage of structures that link candidates with churches"? It is understood that independent and freewill churches are not under an authority that can officially link a candidate with a church. However, strategies can be developed that would increase the likelihood that more churches would be open to consider and call a woman as senior pastor.

To further explore specific examples of strategies that have been used to successfully prepare congregations for female pastors, the male clergy advocates introduced in chapter 7 provide additional recommendations. Bishop Finney and Drs. Rolfs-Massaglia, Lacy, Norwood, and Moss share their experiences, insights, and suggestions.

Preparing for Women Pastors

CS: What steps would you recommend a male pastor take to prepare a congregation to consider a female clergyperson as his successor?

Rev. Dr. Martin Rolfs-Massaglia (Form interview, January 31, 2012, via e-mail)

> Bring women into the pulpit of their church as often as possible; but I think it also begins with the way women are seen by the congregation in general. Since I did not have an associate in my last congregation and since I as a male pastor would be officiating at the Lord's Supper, I used only women to assist me. When we were selecting worship leaders I insisted that there be an equal number of women on the list. In two churches I was instrumental in bringing

women on the deacon board and having them serve communion. How can a congregation consider a woman pastor if women don't have an equal partnership in leadership across the board?

I had little influence in the selection of my successor at my last church, but I did speak to the chair of the search committee and urged him to remember that their job was to find the person God was calling to become pastor, and that they shouldn't allow their perceptions of what the congregation was ready for to impede a thorough search.

Bishop Benjamin G. Finney (In-person interview, January 11, 2012, Cleveland, Ohio)

Teach the Scriptures that show women in leadership positions. Model acceptance. Speak acceptance on a regular basis (no Jew, nor Greek, no males or females . . .). Lift up women in the Scriptures, in song, in prayers.

Rev. Dr. Cleopatrick Lacy (In-person interview, February 4, 2012, Griffin, Georgia)

Take a female associate under their wing and expose her to the boards of the church, give the church board members an opportunity to see her in an official capacity—to see her in the church, functioning and operating. Let her be exposed to the deacon board, trustees, and how they operate. Female clergy need to be invited to church conferences and congregational meetings so they know how things flow.

Rev. Dr. Monte Norwood (Form interview, December 19, 2011, via e-mail)

Regularly, consistently, and clearly teach and proclaim—both publicly and privately—especially with the leadership of the church what Scripture teaches and how the Bible demonstrates the divine intent and biblical call of the usage of all persons, including women, in every area and type of ministry. Show the practical benefit and use of women in areas of society and the community. Further, with concrete examples, intentionally model and utilize female clergypersons in every area of the life and ministry of the parish. Be intentional. Teach. Model. Utilize.

Rev. Dr. Otis Moss Jr. (In-person interview, February 6, 2012, Cleveland, Ohio)

We have to model what we preach and teach and we have to teach it in such a way that no one misses the picture. Even then, there is no guarantee, but if we continue to model, proclaim it, and teach it, bring before the congregation a demonstration of what we are advocating, somewhere that will take root. This may not happen as quickly as it should, but we have to do this in season and out of season. Keep proclaiming this until it becomes not the exception but a part of the general make-up of the community of faith.

CS: Please share any other words of wisdom you have for male pastors, congregations, and search committees concerning calling a woman to the pastorate.

Bishop Benjamin G. Finney

If she can preach—call her. If she can teach—call her. Don't go by the tone of her voice because women don't speak in baritone. God said touch not my anointed and do my prophet no harm. God anoints and calls whom God will.

Here Bishop Finney subtly highlights an unfortunate reality. The tone of the minister's voice has often influenced the call to the pastorate over and above what was being preached or taught. This factor is particularly true in traditions where ministers are expected to whoop (a rhythmic, song-like intonation that is invoked toward the climax of a sermon) or sing a moving song before or after the message. Some congregants are wooed by the tone or sound of a male minister's deep voice, relishing his every word. While some women are able to whoop and sing, many are not. This should not stand in the way of them becoming a senior pastor. As Bishop Finney counsels, if a woman can preach (dividing the Word of God rightly and presenting it in a way that is clear, understandable, and relatable to life), if she can teach (following the principles of correct biblical exegesis and making the Word of God applicable to everyday life), and if she is a person of integrity and intelligence and filled with God's Holy Spirit—call her! Certainly many more skills are needed for pastoral ministry, but the point here is well-taken.

Rev. Dr. Cleopatrick Lacy
> Seek the Lord, pray and the Lord will lead you in the process. If God places a female on your heart, have the courage to accept what God has told you to do.

A search committee may have identified the right candidate based upon qualifications, personality, and discernment. However, committee members may fear repercussions from the congregation or broader community if that candidate happens to be a woman. In addition to much prayer and fasting in the decision-making process, committees can seek the counsel and support of their local denominational leaders. Most will make themselves available to come and speak not only with the committee but also with the congregation, highlighting the strengths and attributes of the candidate, as well as providing examples of success across the nation. Invite the candidate to come and preach a few sermons, teach a Bible study class, or have a time of fellowship over a meal. All of these actions will provide an opportunity for the members to hear the voice of the Lord and look beyond the candidate's gender.

Preparing for the Cost of Transformation

Creating greater opportunities for female clergy to enter the pastorate is a matter not only of changing minds but also of transforming attitudes and ultimately hearts. True transformation can be costly. Individuals who are serious about advocating and strategizing to increase the likelihood that more women will be considered for lead pastorates must be prepared for resistance. Although this point appears obvious, serious consideration, spiritual preparation, and strategic planning for transformation must be a part of any advocacy mission.

In *Twelve Steps to Congregational Transformation*, David C. Laubach suggests that any attempt toward congregational transformation should be accompanied by certain expectations:

> **What You Need to Expect**
> 1. Expect the stress
> 2. Expect the conflict
> 3. Expect the benefits
> 4. Expect the mixed results[2]

Laubach is addressing the topic of congregational transformation. However, for many congregations, a transformation of attitudes, hearts, minds, and spirits is necessary for them to become open to the idea of a woman pastor. Those who would like to prepare the way for such transformation would be wise to prepare for potential resistance. Some congregations have little or no trouble with the idea of having a female pastor. Many, however, do. Laubach shares an example and then offers some important advice for change agents:

> I asked the pastor of a successful turnaround church on Cape Cod to describe the process of change. The most memorable thing he said was that the process was extremely stressful. Even when the transition is viewed as beneficial, change is always stressful, consuming vast resources of time, energy, and talent. In many cases, even the stress of good change becomes a heavy burden, jeopardizing a pastor's physical, emotional, spiritual, and relational health. That risk is even more dramatic when the change is met with resistance. . . . As a leader, expect the stress and prepare for it. Establish a strong support system—one that is not a committee of church members but of persons outside of the congregation.[3]

Those engaged in advocacy on behalf of women in ministry could benefit greatly from dialogue and, if possible, periodic meetings with like-minded individuals. Many a clergyman has accepted and embraced the notion that God can and will call whomever God chooses. However, many have neglected to act upon that belief for fear of angering congregation members, losing revenue, or splitting their church. Many female clergy have been encouraged by their pastors to pursue licensure and ordination in another church or denomination because their pastors are not willing to run the risk of alienating their members.

Pastors taking such a stance are unwittingly endorsing their congregations' rote adherence to tradition rather than developing a sensitivity and spirit of obedience to the voice of the Lord. There are pastors who have taken the risks involved in advocacy for women in ministry and have come out victorious. Although struggles are inevitable and there may be some dissension, following the leading of the Holy Spirit and using wisdom in the preparation process will pay off. Consider the testimony of Dr. Norwood:

> After planting a church in northeast Ohio, serving for thirteen years, and working with women in every area of the ministry, I observed several things. Women were ready, open, and willing to step up and serve as teachers, deacons, and ministers. When the time came for me to transition to another ministry, it was glaringly obvious to me that God had brought to the church, in her first significant church experience, a gifted, conscientious young woman who happened to be a single, black mother who, following her conversion and call experiences, used her 401k to put herself through seminary. At my urging, and in response to our growth and the clear need, she was called as the first full-time associate pastor in the history of the congregation.
>
> When it came time for me to transition out and the search process for the congregation to select a new pastor began, as founding pastor and because of trusted and established relationships, I was able to prayerfully ask the congregation to very seriously pray about and consider whether or not God had sent someone—our female associate pastor who was called, appointed, and anointed—to succeed me and serve as their next senior pastor. The church went through a search, discernment, and selection process. The congregational vote to call her as senior pastor was near unanimous. It did not hurt that she is one of the most gifted preachers and talented administrators I have met. While there were male and female naysayers and those who spoke against this succession and personally gave me strong counsel against this recommendation of

the church calling a female senior pastor, God has blessed the succession.

The church's prophetic witness has dramatically increased, and the congregation has nearly doubled in size and continues to grow and thrive. I share this hoping that other pastors will both look within their congregations and intentionally include female clergy involved in their search process—including as viable candidates with as much or more to offer as any male.

If only more fathers in the ministry had this kind of vision and courage! Several strategies that Dr. Norwood employed are especially noteworthy:

■ Intentionally place qualified women in areas of practical ministry: Bible study teachers, the deacon board, and associate ministers.
■ If possible financially, hire a female to fill ministerial staff positions beyond the traditional roles of Christian educator or nursery director.
■ Nurture an environment of trust for pastoral leaders on all levels (don't allow insecurities to cause you to undermine the trust that develops between congregation and staff as healthy communication, respect, and support grows).
■ Don't allow naysayers to stop you from following the voice and leading of God's Holy Spirit regarding recommending a woman.

When a pulpit becomes vacant, churches also need to be prayerful, seek guidance from denominational leaders, and be open to new possibilities, as Dr. Moss observes:

> Search committees are not engines for social change. They can do a lot of damage if they are not carefully presented. Sometimes search committees do more damage in the

process and set congregations back. We can get carried away with the number of applications. I do not think that is a good way of doing a pastoral search. The best search committee goes out and searches for a person prayerfully who can bring to the congregation and community great leadership, not saying "we are such and such a church and folks would love to come here!" So many times the best candidate won't even send in an application.

Dr. Moss also stressed the importance for departing pastors to prepare their congregations for the transition. Insecurity and the need to hold on often hinder the preparation process.

We have to prepare congregations in advance if we are leaving. We need to prepare people for that inevitable moment when a transition will take place. Often we are insecure, so busy trying to hold on. We are not free enough to do the necessary things for a prayerful, creative, and productive transition. Leadership has the responsibility of modeling before the congregation what is available, what they ought to be open to long before that moment arrives.

Because we are not in the episcopacy where the bishop says, "This is your next pastor," the Baptist model is great and dangerous at the same time. It is dangerous because a handful of people can become the spokespersons for hundreds or even thousands and be totally unqualified. It's great because it has the potential of doing an honorable service. Often it is muffled and politicized. People begin to bargain and cut deals, hoping that if this person comes, then [that person] will be part of the inner circle. It is an imperfect process that can rise above all of the petty frailties, now and then coming through with a prophet.

Several nuggets of wisdom can be harvested from Dr. Moss's counsel.

■ Search committees must avoid getting "carried away" with the number of applications. Rather than relying upon applications, committee members may need to go and search prayerfully (hence the title "search committee") for the best candidate.

■ Often the best candidate will not send in an application. Again, denominational leaders such as an executive minister or area minister may be able to provide the names of individuals who may fit the congregational needs. Some denominations such as the American Baptists have a profile system that can be accessed to match congregational needs with candidates.

■ Pastors should prepare congregations before leaving. Pastors should ask the Lord to deliver them from insecurities that imprison them and keep them from strategically developing a "creative and productive" transition plan.

■ Through prayer and wise counsel, search committees and churches should do their utmost to avoid allowing the pastoral search process to become politicized.

Strengths and Benefits That Women Bring to Pastoral Ministry

Consider a just a few of the strengths and benefits that women bring to the pastoral ministry.

Women tend to multitask effectively. Often wearing multiple hats of wife, mother, daughter, pastor, counselor, teacher, and administrator, women tend to be able to compartmentalize their lives in such a way that each segment is well cared for. Although this skill can be a danger to the woman, with wisdom and the fine art of delegation, her multitasking skills can serve her and her congregation very well.

Women pastors can be role models for young women. When so many young women look to unrealistic and doctored images in magazines and on the silver screen, a strong, intelligent, Holy-Spirit filled woman standing before them each Sunday, delivering a message of hope, redemption, and assurance, can go a long way to counteract the damaging images of today's society. A woman pastor can also show young men that strong women should not be feared or avoided but admired, respected, honored, and cherished.

Women can more easily provide pastoral care in certain settings. It is much easier for a female pastor to make hospital calls to women parishioners who may be concerned about their appearance (stages of undress, messy hair, and no make-up). It also may be easier for some male parishioners to share their apprehensions and fears with a woman whose nurturing spirit frees them from having to maintain the stiff upper lip they may feel compelled to show to a male pastor.

Women highlight the feminine attributes of God's love. Natural nurturers, women can bring a softer side to the pastorate. They tend to be great listeners, consider each side of an argument carefully, discern the nuances of exhibited behaviors, and act accordingly. Being a woman, she can readily detect when other women (who most probably make up the majority of the congregation) are manifesting certain characteristics due to insecurities, jealousies, or esteem issues. If she embraces her femininity rather than trying to act like a male (dressing like a man, imitating male preachers), she can win over even her staunchest male critics with her beautiful composure.

Women tend to have stronger interpersonal skills. Women tend to have a keener sense of awareness about feelings and emotions and when, where, and how to address matters. For this reason, male and female parishioners may find it easier to share confidences, express frustrations, and reveal inner feelings to a woman pastor. Women appear to find it easier to give praise, highlight positive attributes of others verbally, and write notes of appreciation. Women also seem to more readily show compassion and consider how others may feel as a factor in decisions they make.

Rev. Maria Khaleel shares the following insight about women and communication skills:

> One contribution that women bring to the table is in the area of communication. Women are naturally more communicative than men. This is an excellent quality in leadership. But we have to make sure this is under the control of the Holy Spirit.
>
> Deborah called for Barak, the military general leader of Israel. She did not just say, "Go to battle," but she explained to him the Word of the Lord. She explained the strategy. She explained what the outcome would be. She wasn't directive; she was relational. And that is powerful as far as leadership skill is concerned. In leadership training you learn that knowledge is empowering. The more people know, the more they will function well in their position or their task. So we can communicate knowledge because we are communicators. Men are more the just-do-it type, "because I said so."[4]

The characteristics that women bring to any leadership endeavor should not be viewed as reasons to choose a woman instead of a man but rather as reasons to be open-minded and conscious of the benefits that may be overlooked due to stereotypes, rigid mindsets, and gender prejudice.

Throughout this work, female and male pastors have shared from their wealth of experiences guiding principles that can help to encourage, caution, empower, and instruct women called to pastoral ministry. Here is an overview of what was shared.

■ Remember that Jesus had women in his ministry circle. How can a congregation consider a pastor if women aren't in leadership across the board?

■ Adopt female seminarians to work as associates in the church. Reach out to male colleagues and ask them to offer preaching opportunities for major events (revivals, Sunday morning).

■ Bring women into leadership as often as possible.

■ Be open to the Lord's answer even though it may not be what you want to hear.

■ Male pastors need to help women develop their shield of faith in the broader community.

■ Guard against selecting unqualified males and overlooking super-qualified females.

■ Model what you preach and teach, and teach in such a way that no one misses it.

■ Model, practice, and teach your belief about advocating for women.

■ Search committees must pray and seek professional guidance (such as executive or area ministers). They must have the courage to obey God's voice over against naysayers.

Ruth B. Minter offers this insight:

> In the long run, however, churches will ignore a candidate's gender only if our faith communities become substantially more involved in nurturing the whole humanity of both their women and their men. The church must nourish sources of friendship and support and expand the possibilities for developing feelings of self-esteem and self-worth—for both sexes and all ages. Then, secure in the community of faith, the children of God will be able to see God's gifts in each other and to share tasks according to those gifts, without allowing hidden psychological needs to block their understanding of where the Holy Spirit would have them move.[5]

Joel 2:28 (NIV) declares, "And afterward, I will pour out my Spirit on all people. Your sons and daughters will prophesy." The sovereignty of God positions God to select those whom God chooses to proclaim the good news about salvation through Jesus Christ. Women and men are anointed by God to preach the Word in season and out of season. Women and men are called by God to mend the brokenhearted, to open blinded eyes, and to set at liberty those who are oppressed (Luke 4:18). Human frailty, fraught with jealousies, insecurities, hunger for power, and the need to promote self, has created stained glass ceilings. Beyond the ceiling, however, the brightness of God's glory, grace, strength, and hope awaits. Beyond dogma, beyond traditions based upon poor exegesis, beyond the violence of oppression, and beyond cosmetic unity lies the assignment God has given pastors to seek and to save that which was lost. If male and female pastors will do these things, they will have the faith, the courage, the strategies, and the perseverance to break through and rise beyond the stained glass ceiling.

Notes

1. Edward C. Lehman Jr., "Women's Path into Ministry: Six Major Studies," in *Pulpit and Pew Research on Pastoral Leadership Reports* (Durham, NC: Duke Divinity School, 2002), 19.

2. David C. Laubach, *Twelve Steps to Congregational Transformation: A Practical Guide for Leaders* (Valley Forge, PA: Judson Press, 2006), 49.

3. Laubach, *Twelve Steps to Congregational Transformation,* 50.

4. Maria Khaleel, "Strength in Diversity: Working with an All-Male Team," The Assemblies of God Network for Women in Ministry, ag.org/wim/resources/articles/misc/misc0309_01wim Khaleel.cfm (accessed November 24, 2012).

5. Ruth Brandon Minter, "Hidden Dynamics Block Women's

Access to Pulpits," *Christian Century*, August 29–September 5, 1994, 805.

Words of Wisdom for Women Clergy

■ Always have somebody in your life to hold you accountable and always be under the covering of somebody who loves God. Have a mentor.

■ Have a safe place where you can go to be ministered to and have a time of rest. Seek spiritual mothers and fathers who will help when we need counsel.

■ Avoid going to parishioners with personal issues.

■ Avoid pre-judging. Stop the misconceptions that we might have about one another simply because we don't know one another. A spirit of authenticity is needed to break down barriers.

■ Seek to come under the tutelage of someone who will endorse you. Remember, your gifts will make room for you.

■ Look for a role model who can mold bright minds without stifling creativity.

■ Constantly renew your mind. Stay focused and study God's Word.

■ Seminary is a must. Do not be fearful of the seminary experience.

■ Keep the vision out in front of you so you will stay excited and less likely to wander from the original plan. Wait on the Lord and his timing.

■ Don't be envious of other ministries because that is like having weak ankles.

■ God needs you to be yourself. You do you!

■ Stay in your own lane. Don't drift when you drive. Minister from your own position.

■ You have to deal with your own issues and insecurities before you can help others.

■ Be open to non-traditional places to minister outside of the church. This will open more doors for you and give you exposure.

■ Bond with other women and men who offer fellowship, dialogue, and from time to time opportunities to grow in ministry.

■ Allow yourself to be engaged in endeavors beyond the local church. Seek a definition that is larger than just the pastorate. The pastorate is a very important and sacred calling, but not the Alpha and Omega of Ministry.

Recommended Reading

Bristow, John T. *What Paul Really Said about Women: The Apostle's Liberating Views on Equality in Marriage, Leadership, and Love.* New York: HarperCollins, 1991.

Clouse, Bonnidell, and Robert G. Clouse, eds. *Women in Ministry: Four Views.* Downers Grove, IL: InterVarsity Press, 1989.

Earls, Denvis O. *Daughters of God: Southern Baptist Women in the Pulpit: Heresy vs. the Call to Preach.* Frederick, MD: PublishAmerica, 2006.

Harris, Mamie. *Detour to Destiny.* Huntley, IL: Mall Publishing, 2008.

Johnson, Wilma R. *Giving Away My Joy: The Psalmist Model of Spiritual Joy: A Commentary on Pastoral Leadership.* Lithonia, GA: Orman Press, 2005.

Johnson Cook, Suzan. *Becoming a Woman of Destiny: Turning Life's Trials into Triumphs.* New York: Tarcher, 2010.

Laubach, David C. *Twelve Steps to Congregational Transformation: A Practical Guide for Leaders.* Valley Forge, PA: Judson Press, 2006.

McKenzie, Vashti. *Not Without a Struggle: Leadership Development for African American Women in Ministry.* Cleveland: Pilgrim Press, 2011.

Moore, Allison M. *Clergy Moms: A Survival Guide to Balancing Family and Congregation.* New York: Seabury, 2008.

Mosley, Denise. *Can I Go Beyond the Veil? The Burning Controversy for Many Women of God in the Baptist Church Today.* Frederick, MD: PublishAmerica, 2005.

Purvis, Sally B. *The Stained-Glass Ceiling: Churches and Their Women Pastors.* Louisville: Westminster John Knox, 1995.

Shepastor blogsite. http://shepastor.blogspot.com.

Walker, Riley, and Marcia Patton. *When the Spirit Moves: A Guide for Ministers in Transition.* Valley Forge, PA: Judson Press, 2011.

Wolfe, James Owen, III. *American Baptist Women in Pastoral Ministry: A Contemporary Survey.* South Bend, IN: Cloverdale Books, 2007.

Zikmund, Barbara Brown, Adair T. Lummis, and Patricia M. Y. Chang. *Clergy Women: An Uphill Calling.* Louisville: Westminster John Knox, 1998.

About the Author

A native of Akron, Ohio, the Reverend Christine A. Smith accepted Jesus Christ as her personal savior at the age of fifteen. She answered the call to ministry and was licensed to preach in the Tabernacle Baptist Church of Akron, Ohio, at age seventeen. She holds a bachelor of science in education, specializing in learning disabilities and developmental handicaps from the University of  Akron (1987). She holds a master of divinity from the Interdenominational Theological Center, Morehouse School of Religion in Atlanta, Georgia, specializing in systematic theology and women's studies (1990). In 1993 Rev. Smith joined the Olivet Institutional Baptist Church in Cleveland, Ohio, under the pastorate of the Reverend Dr. Otis Moss Jr., and was ordained to the gospel ministry in 1995. She served Olivet as minister of Christian education for three years. Rev. Smith was featured in *The African American Pulpit* as one of the "Twenty to Watch" (Winter 2001–2002, Judson Press).

In January 2006, Rev. Smith became pastor of the Covenant Baptist Church in Wickliffe, Ohio. She holds the distinction of becoming the first female pastor of Covenant, the first African American pastor of Covenant, and the second female Baptist pastor of a mainline denomination in the greater Cleveland area

(American Baptist Churches USA). She currently serves as president of the board of trustees of the Cleveland Baptist Association. In 2009 Rev. Smith wrote and successfully secured a grant from the National Ministers Council (ABCUSA) to begin Women Together in Ministry (WTIM) of Greater Cleveland. WTIM is a network designed to connect, encourage, and support women in ministry. She also produces a weekly blog, Shepastor (http://shepastor.blog spot.com), a site dedicated to providing encouragement, guidance, words of wisdom, and instruction to female clergy. In March 2012 the Cleveland *Plain Dealer* featured her article "Being Persistent in Pursuit of Social Justice" in the *Messages of Faith* column.

Rev. Smith is proud wife of Aristide Smith Jr. and blessed mother of three wonderful children: two sons, Aristide III and Caleb, and a daughter, Aris Christine. Truly, God has been good to the Reverend Christine A. Smith. For the Lord's loving kindness and tender mercies, she simply says, "To God be the glory for the things he has done!"